CRITICAL ISSUES IN CARIBBEAN DEVELOPMENT

Number 1

West Indian Development and the Deepening and Widening of the Caribbean Community

CRITICAL ISSUES IN
CARIBBEAN DEVELOPMENT

Number 1   West Indian Development and the Deepening and
              Widening of the Caribbean Community
              William G. Demas

Number 2   The New World Trade Order: Uruguay Round
              Agreements and Implications for CARICOM States
              Frank Rampersad et al

Number 3   Institutional Aspects of West Indian Development
              Jones, Mills, Henry, LeFranc et al

CRITICAL ISSUES IN CARIBBEAN DEVELOPMENT

Number 1

West Indian Development and the Deepening and Widening of the Caribbean Community

William G. Demas

Ian Randle Publishers
and
Institute of Social and Economic Research (ISER)
University of the West Indies

Published in Jamaica 1997 by
Ian Randle Publishers
206 Old Hope Road,
Kingston 6,
Jamaica W.I.

© 1997 William G. Demas

All rights reserved – no part of this publication may be reproduced, stored in a retrieval system, or transmitted in any form, or by any means electronic, photocopying, recording or otherwise without the prior permission of the author or publisher.

ISBN 976-8123-02-8

A catalogue record for this book is available from the National Library of Jamaica.

Cover and book design by Robert Harris
Set in 9.5/14 Janson x 27
Printed in Jamaica by Stephenson's Litho Press

To my Mother

and

To the West Indian Political Leaders who signed the Treaty of Chaguaramas establishing The Caribbean Community (CARICOM)

and

To the West Indian Political Leaders who signed the Treaty of Basse Terre establishing The Organization of Eastern Caribbean States (OECS)

and

To the West Indian Political Leaders, Ministers, Parliamentarians the other Social Partners, National and Regional Public Servants, Intellectuals, Mass Media Personnel and all other West Indians who supported, and continue to support, West Indian Development, Integration and Sovereignty and Wider Caribbean Integration and Cooperation

Contents

Foreword / *viii*

Acknowledgements / *ix*

Acronyms and Abbreviations / *xi*

Introduction / *xiii*

1 West Indian Development in a Rapidly Changing World Economy / *1*

2 The need for a Transition to greater Self-Reliance and International Competitiveness / *18*

3 The Rationale of Integration and the Essentials of CARICOM / *22*

4 The Grand Anse Declaration and the Establishment of the West Indian Commission / *33*

5 Clarification of CARICOM Issues / *36*

6 The Deepening of the Caribbean Community / *48*

7 The LDCs, The OECs and the Caribbean Development Bank / *62*

8 The Widening of the Caribbean Community / *66*

9 Towards a Coordinated External Trade Policy for the Caribbean Community / *77*

10 A Cautiously Optimistic View of the West Indies Over the next two Decades / *90*

Postscript / *92*

Appendix A: Grand Anse Declaration and Work Programme for the Advancement of the Integration Movement / *117*

Appendix B: Statistical Tables on Economies of the Caribbean Community and the Wider Caribbean / *120*

Appendix C: Some Formal Statements on CARICOM by Heads of Government and State / *133*

Appendix D: References and Additional Material / *135*

Foreword

I am very pleased to write this brief Foreword for a number of studies undertaken under the Project jointly sponsored and funded by the Andrew Mellon Foundation, the Caribbean Development Bank and the Institute of Social and Economic Research (ISER), University of the West Indies.

Some fourteen research projects were undertaken between 1993 and 1995. Some of them have been put together to form the subject-matter of some of these books, others will be presented or made available as Research Studies or Working Papers.

The subject-matter of the set of studies undertaken under the Project is Critical Issues in Caribbean Development. As agreed with the Mellon Foundation, the work was broadly coordinated by myself as Vice-Chancellor and the Directors of ISER at St Augustine, Cave Hill and Mona. The Project Director, the Honorable William Demas, was based at ISER, Mona.

The first conference was held five months after the start of the project and the second near the end of the Project. I would like to thank the Andrew Mellon Foundation, the Caribbean Development Bank and all of those persons who were either directly or indirectly associated with this Project.

The studies are now being shared with the wider public of the region and with the decision-makers in both the public and the private sectors so that informed opinions on various economic and trade options facing the Caribbean Community and its member states in meeting the several challenges ahead, can be generated.

SIR ALISTER McINTYRE
Vice Chancellor
The University of the West Indies
May 9, 1996.

Acknowledgements

This work was undertaken as part of the Andrew Mellon Foundation Project grant to the University of the West Indies (UWI) to study critical issues in Caribbean development, with emphasis on external economic relations and on policy choices facing governments. The Caribbean Development Bank also deserves thanks for the speedy manner in which they responded so that certain further work on the the Project may be conducted.

I would like to express my deep appreciation to the Andrew Mellon Foundation, the Caribbean Development Bank and the University of the West Indies for making the entire project possible.

I must acknowledge the helpful comments on the first rough draft of the paper by Sir Shridath Ramphal and Sir Alister McIntyre, Chancellor and Vice-Chancellor respectively of the University of the West Indies.

I am also grateful for the useful and constructive comments I received from: Marius St Rose, Vice-President of the Caribbean Development Bank; Kari Levitt, Professor of Economics of the Consortium Graduate School of the University of the West Indies at Mona; Professor Bisnodat Persaud, Director of UWI Centre for Environment and Development; Dwight Venner, Governor of the Central Bank of the Eastern Caribbean States; Ambassador Don Brice, formerly Director-General of the West Indian Commission; Dr Alvin Hilaire, Senior Advisor in the Central Bank of Trinidad and Tobago; and Dr Leith Dunn, Director of CUSO in Jamaica.

Acknowledgements are also due to Sir Neville Nicholls, President of the Caribbean Development Bank, Dr Edwin Carrington and Byron Blake, Secretary-General and Assistant Secretary-General respectively of the Caribbean Community, who permitted me access to data from their organisations. Earl Baccus was also helpful on the matter of the information industry and other services. A special word of thanks is due to Hubert Williams, Information Officer of the CDB, for his excellent editing of the penultimate version of the text.

Mention must also be made of the support I received from Dr Elsie LeFranc and Dr Helen McBain, Director and Deputy Director respectively of the Institute of Social and Economic Research (ISER, Mona), and from Gloria Burke, Office Manager, Judith Tavares, Project Administrator and all the other staff members of the Institute, especially an intelligent and able young man, Floyd Williams. Audrey Wood also did an excellent job in preparing the first draft of this book.

It would be ungracious of me not to mention the full and active cooperation of Audrey Chambers and Norma Davis, Head and Deputy Head respectively of the Documentation/Data Centre of ISER, and from Annie Paul, Publications Editor of ISER.

WILLIAM G. DEMAS
Director,
UWI/Andrew Mellon Foundation/CDB Project
Institute of Social and Economic Research
University of the West Indies (Mona), Jamaica
May, 1996

Acronyms and Abbreviations

ACP	African, Caribbean and Pacific (countries; referring to Lomé Convention)
ACS	Association of Caribbean States;
ASEAN	Association of South-east Asian Nations
CACM	Central American Common Market
CAIC	Caribbean Association of Industry and Commerce
CANA	Caribbean News Agency
CARDI	Caribbean Agricultural Research Development Institute
CARIBCAN	Caribbean-Canadian Trade Agreement
CARICOM	Caribbean Community
CARIFESTA	Caribbean Festival of Arts
CARIFTA	Caribbbean Free Trade Association
CARTIS	CARICOM Trade and Information Service
CBI	Caribbean Basin Initiative
CBU	Caribbean Broadcasting Union
CDB	Caribbean Development Bank
CEDP	Caribbean Export Development Project
CER	Common Enterprise Regime
CET	Common External Tariff
CGCED	Caribbean Group for Co-operation in Economic Development
CIC	Caribbean Investment Corporation
CIPS	Caribbean Industrial Programming Scheme
CMCF	CARICOM Multilateral Clearing Facility
ECCB	Eastern Caribbean Central Bank
ECLAC	Economic Council for Latin America and the Caribbean
ECOWAS	Economic Community of West African States
EDF	European Development Bank
EIB	European Investment Bank
EV	European Vision

FAO	UN Food and Agriculture Organisation
FTAA	Free Trade Area of the Americas
GSP	Generalised System of Preferences
IDB	replace with IADB, Inter-American Development Bank
IMF	International Monetary Fund
LDC	Less Developed Countries
MDC	More Developed Countries
NAFTA	North Americian Free Trade Agreement
NGO	Non-governmental Organisation
OAS	Organisation of African States
OECS	Organisation of Eastern Caribbean States
PAHO	Pan-American Health Organisation
UNDP	United Nations Development Programme
UNICEF	United Nations
WTO	World Trade Organization

Introduction

To date the conference of heads of government of the Caribbean Community (CARICOM) has accepted many of the recommendations of the West Indian Commission with respect to the strengthening of the Community via the creation of a single market (economic union) and the widening of CARICOM through trade and economic relations in neighbouring non-English-speaking Caribbean countries.

This book explores the deepening of CARICOM especially with respect to the goal of the single market. The Commission recommended the acceleration of the process of functional cooperation and the establishment of common services, particularly a West Indian Court of Appeal. It called for greater coordination of foreign policies, including external trade policies, and the setting up where feasible, of joint CARICOM embassies abroad.

In light of the underlying nature of West Indian economies and the trends towards globalisation and regionalism, CARICOM is seen as an essential element in promoting international competitiveness, greater self-reliance and West Indian identity. The alternatives to a strengthened CARICOM are either 'marginalisation' or *de jure* or *de facto* 'absorption' in a highly dependent mode into one or more much bigger and more powerful country or group of countries.

The positive case for CARICOM is well-known: helping our countries to achieve economies of scale and critical mass in many economic and non-economic activities; the facilitation of extra-regional exports and efficient regional import substitution; functional cooperation and common services in a wide range of fields; and the achievement of greater bargaining power vis-à-vis the outside world.

Development appropriate to the region is defined as efficient economic growth combined with social equity. This includes the promotion of enterprises of all scales combined with the alleviation of poverty and the significant reduction of unemployment.

SOME BASIC PREMISES

1. CARICOM's stance with respect to itself as well as to its long-standing preferential agreements with metropolitan countries must be placed in the context of recent movements towards a hemispheric free trade area. It is considered that for the CARICOM countries the Free Trade Area of the Americas (FTAA) is an alternative to the expansion of NAFTA in that the FTAA permits CARICOM and other sub-regional integration movements to maintain and strengthen the links among their member countries and between themselves and other sub-regional integration groupings (including NAFTA) in the hemisphere.
2. Previous trade agreements – for example, with the European Union under the Lomé Convention – would not be seen as being in conflict with the FTAA but as providing a much wider market for export development and competitive strengthening, provided that reciprocity remains selective and not applied across the board.
3. New relationships such as the Association of Caribbean States (ACS) increase, not decrease, the imperative towards stronger CARICOM integration. Thus membership in the ACS does not negate the importance of CARICOM. The ACS is about cooperation in trade, investment, finance, tourism, transport, science, technology, education, health, culture, etc. Deep integration such as a single market or economic union is not practical at this stage for the ACS. A practical approach over time to deep economic integration (involving ultimately full membership of CARICOM) might be more feasible between CARICOM and one, two or three of the non-English-speaking independent islands of the Greater Antilles.
4. The 'shield' of CARICOM is necessary to provide some degree of effective sovereignty for the individual CARICOM countries and help them to secure greater benefits from external trade and other economic and diplomatic relationships through joint external negotiations and bargaining. Should CARICOM countries attempt to negotiate individually, the Community might disintegrate. The result would be not only a loss of diplomatic and economic strength but of vital intangibles such as international credibility and a sense of West Indian community and identity.

KEY ISSUES

1. Should market integration go beyond a single market, that is, intra-CARICOM free trade; a truly common external tariff, (CET), complete factor mobility in the medium and long term; consultation on and coordination of national economic policies; and financial and monetary cooperation and integration

(including the establishment of fixed exchange rates between national currencies and a single currency)? The answer is yes. First, there is a crying need for cooperation in joint investments as between the private sectors of the member countries. Second, the need for cooperation in production and in both intra- and extra-regional marketing should be emphasised.

Cooperation in investment and, more generally, in production and marketing requires an active private sector and is complementary to a common economic space. This cooperation includes strategies such as the integration of production as between national economies, joint ventures across countries as well as a regional industrial and agricultural policy complemented by an appropriate legal and regulatory regional framework. Joint marketing, both within and outside CARICOM, could be undertaken by private-sector trading companies.

2. How can CARICOM in this age of trade liberalisation and open regionalism be of use to its member countries? It should provide an environment conducive to export-oriented development policies as well as efficient regional import substitution. These policies should focus on internal and external macroeconomic stabilisation, increasing productivity, higher levels of domestic savings and productive sector investment, human resource development, etc. They all add up to the facilitation of the international competitiveness of the CARICOM economies, of critical importance to the strengthening of the productive sectors. It should be emphasised that the most important factor in achieving West Indian international competitiveness is increasing productivity. This involves many policies, programmes and measures, the chief of which is human resource development.

3. The relationship between deepening and widening is crucial. The deepening of CARICOM must be achieved in order to make widening and closer trade cooperation with much bigger and more powerful countries, near and far, workable.

4. What form should the widening of CARICOM take? Widening in the form of closer relations with our neighbours is possible on the basis of: trade; financial and economic cooperation; collaboration in science, technology, culture; and in education and training. This is bound to develop into an intensive and extensive programme of practical economic and technical cooperation. There may also in the medium to long term be a degree of hemispheric free trade under the FTAA. Full membership of CARICOM over the medium to long term can be envisaged for one or more of the Greater Antillean islands.

5. The historical and current pattern of West Indian development has been one of dependence on preferences in metropolitan markets as exemplified by regimes of non-reciprocal preferences and heavy dependence on external

financial assistance. Our economies need to become less externally dependent and more self-reliant, that is to say, more internationally competitive. How can this be effected? We need to redouble urgently our economic efforts to do everything listed above. But even with tremendous internal efforts, we need a period of transition before we can become internationally competitive. During this transition we need external help to promote self-help on our part.

CONCLUSIONS

1. CARICOM should be deepened and become of increasing importance to us while as a united body we develop relationships of cooperation with the larger Latin American and other hemispheric countries and sub-regional groups (including NAFTA), as well as economic blocs further afield, particularly the European Union. Membership of either the ACS or CARICOM is not the issue. CARICOM remains essential to us and there is enormous scope for practical cooperation between a deepened CARICOM and the ACS. Indeed deepening is a condition for the widening of CARICOM.
2. CARICOM countries need time and continued external support if they are to successfully complete the transition towards being internationally competitive, resilient and more self-reliant. This should be given due recognition by hemispheric and West European preference-giving governments as well as multilateral and bilateral donors. The nature of the West Indian economy as a result of our historical legacy is such that at this crucial juncture we need for another fifteen years continuing non-reciprocal preferences and external aid.

1

West Indian Development in a Rapidly Changing World Economy[1]

BRIEF AND BROAD OVERVIEW OF THE WEST INDIAN ECONOMIC SITUATION

The fundamental point about our economies is that they have always had a strong export orientation. Indeed, the West Indies is the earliest third-world economy, having been integrated into the European economies during the sixteenth and seventeenth centuries mainly in order to export sugar to Europe. More recently cocoa, coffee and bananas emerged here as important crops. In this century we have become exporters of petroleum, bauxite and alumina, and of course tourism. The West Indies needs to become more export-oriented, particularly in the manufacturing sector, which is the sole sector which has not been export-oriented. It also needs to become more self-sufficient (but obviously not totally so) in food.

We are high-cost producers of traditional agricultural exports like sugar and bananas but we can continue producing only with the support of preferences available in the markets of the European Union (EU) and the USA.

Because we are not sufficiently competitive in our exports of manufactures, agro-industries and non-traditional agricultural products, we are unable to make full use of our duty-free access for those items to the markets of the EU under the Lomé Convention, the USA under the CBI and Canada under CARIBCAN. We have in the past not been required to give tariff reciprocity to the countries which give us preferences under Lomé, the CBI and CARIBCAN.

In some of our countries there is still need for economic stabilisation and external debt relief.

We have over the last fifteen years received large amounts of bilateral donor country and multilateral development assistance and other forms of official financial inflows which have been high on a per head basis. A major factor in the high levels per head of aid has been the operation since the late 1970s of the Caribbean Group for Cooperation in Economic Development (CGCED), coordinated by the World Bank, and the Caribbean Development Bank supported by the CDB. But perhaps a more fundamental factor has been that in small and very small countries much of the infrastructure is subject to 'indivisibilities' and therefore has a high cost per head of population. There is a lack of critical mass for many infrastructure products and research and administrative services in small and very small economies.

Although real incomes (in US dollars) per head have grown in the Organisation of Eastern Caribbean States (OECS), the Bahamas and Belize, all the economies remain structurally weak and undiversified in both production and exports and rely heavily on imported food and animal feeds. In many countries there are high levels of unemployment and some poverty.

We are frequently the victims of natural disasters such as flooding, high winds and hurricanes, and drought. Because of our small size, these disasters can affect entire countries.

Let us now focus on some of our problems:

First, high-cost West Indian traditional export products such as sugar and particularly bananas may lose their preferential markets in Europe. We need to:

- reduce unit costs of production in all sectors of the economy, especially those producing tradeable goods and services;
- develop more remunerative by-products of our existing traditional agricultural commodities; and
- change the existing predominant end-use of the agricultural crops being grown.

All these are more easily said than done.

Second, we have not developed exports of agro-industries and manufactured goods (neither of segmented production nor of specialties for niche markets) at competitive prices and of the necessary standards, quality and reliability of delivery. (The establishment of export Free Zones should not be ruled out for those few West Indian countries which can produce labour-intensive goods at low costs).

Third, we have not yet been able to any great extent to export to the outside world non-traditional agricultural products such as tropical fruit, ground provisions, winter vegetables, tropical foliage and cut flowers.

Fourth, we are not yet making a sufficiently great effort to develop exports to extra-CARICOM markets of non-tourism foreign exchange earning services, such as engineering, architectural, economic and financial consultancies, construction contracts, computer software, financial services, telecommunications, informatics, educational and medical/recreational services.

Fifth, there are bad shortfalls in food production (as well as animal feeds) for both local and regional markets, resulting in reliance on massive imports of both.

Sixth, we need to make greater efforts to put in place mechanisms to increase our rates of domestic savings (private-sector, public-sector and household), in view of the near certainty of a decline in both development aid and private financial flows into our countries.

THE RAPIDLY CHANGING WORLD ECONOMY

West Indians cannot afford to ignore the changes taking place in the global international, economic, technological and political environment which are already affecting most countries in the world.

One of these is the segmentation of production, locating different parts of the production process in different parts of the world, depending on the levels of skills, wage rates, the productivity of labour, transport costs, etc. At the same time economies of scale have become less important in certain kinds of production.

There is a global trend towards privatisation of ownership of public utilities and directly productive state enterprises. The reasons for this are twofold: the observed manifest failure of central planning in the former Soviet Union and other East European countries; and the fact that in most developing countries state ownership of public utilities and state enterprises has not yielded good results.

We need to list the major changes now taking place in the world economy.

1. The globalisation of corporate production leading to segmentation of production in different countries of the world. This results in the location of different parts or segments of production in different parts of the world, depending on the level of skills, wage rates, productivity of labour, transport costs, etc. At the same time, with the development of niche markets for specialised products, economies of scale have become less important in certain kinds of production, but by no means all.
2. The growth of world trade at a faster rate than world production.
3. The growing tendency throughout the world towards the liberalisation of international trade in goods and services and, with the success of the recently concluded Uruguay Round, the possibility of a much strengthened GATT (now WTO).
4. The growing importance of both tourism and non-tourism services in their shares of world trade.
5. The growing element of high-technology services in manufactured goods.
6. A growing trend towards participation of the private sector in the ownership of state enterprises and public utilities.

7. The likelihood of a continuing decline in development assistance to developing countries and likely increase of such flows to former Communist countries and to Africa.
8. The globalisation of finance in the sense that 24 hours a day billions of dollars of finance move around the main financial centres of the world in response to marginal or expected changes in exchange rates and interest rates.
9. Intensified competition not only in price but also in product differentiation, in standards, quality and reliability of delivery in world trade.
10. The emergence of regional (or continental) mega-blocs in trade, mainly the EU and NAFTA (with the strong likelihood of an East Asian bloc, including Japan and the East Asian outstanding performers), and (perhaps) China, Australia, New Zealand and some other South Asian countries.
11. The corresponding tendency of much smaller and more closely knit sub-regional groupings to be formed or to be reinvigorated. The list of these latter is long: CARICOM, the Central American Common Market, the Andean Group, ASEAN and East and Central African PTA, and the Economic Community of West African States (ECOWAS). Mercosur (comprising Argentina, Brazil, Paraguay and Uruguay) now exists. In addition to inter-group free trade the establishment of a Common External Tariff (CET) is a priority. The Association of Caribbean States (ACS) is the most recently formed economic and technical cooperation group (Globalisation of the world economy is not, after all as novel as it is made out to be. The process stated with Europe's arrival in the New World around the year 1500. In addition, with the former European colonies completely politically independent, the issue of global governance to deal with the globalised world economy will in our view soon become one of growing importance.)

Some of the policy measures and development strategies which the rapidly changing world environment has imposed on us in CARICOM would have become inevitable. Our economic difficulties are attitudinal, structural and institutional and are the result of centuries of external political and economic control. The rapid pace of global change means that we have to accelerate our efforts to overcome our problems.

The West Indian economies need to become much more efficient and internationally competitive, as well as more resilient and more diversified in both production and exports, thus undergoing structural transformation.

ECONOMIC AND OTHER FORMS OF VULNERABILITY

The region is not only vulnerable in its economic structure and in terms of national disasters. It is also vulnerable in terms of political and diplomatic power. This is especially pertinent when member states of CARICOM try to act on an individual basis. It is susceptible to the trade and transshipment of narcotic drugs to North America and western Europe.

POSITIVE FACTORS IN WEST INDIAN DEVELOPMENT[2]

For the West Indies all is not doom and gloom. We should look at the present world situation positively and become proactive rather than reactive. Structural transformation of our economies entails shifting to a more flexible and diversified production and exports, and bringing underutilised resources of land and labour into productive employment. Some efforts are already being made in this direction by a few entrepreneurs, which should make it easy for others to follow. Private-sector groups as well as governments understand that if we do not now make the efforts required to straighten out our economies, we will probably never be able to do so again.

If structural transformation is to progress it will be necessary to achieve and maintain macro-economic stability as soon as possible and to win additional external debt relief. A problem here is that multilateral financial institutions do not reschedule debt owing to them. The creditor and debtor countries should join forces to seek a significant reduction of this debt. One may even argue that the very heavy burden of servicing external debt has contributed more to the long drawn out agony of many of the poorer people in two of the most populous countries of CARICOM. It would of course violate the spirit of CARICOM if significant volumes of intra-regional debt were not serviced in accordance with agreed schedules.

There are some grounds for optimism about West Indian economic prospects. One is the response of the small-scale informal sector in Guyana and Jamaica to the economic opportunities presented by the very difficult economic and social conditions in the late 1970s and the 1980s. Another is the plethora of opportunities for small-scale and medium enterprises to export specialty items with a West Indian flavour and appearance for niche markets abroad.

There are many possibilities for what Auliana Poon has termed "axial" tourism, which brings about vertical, horizontal and diagonal linkages between tourism and other sectors (producing both products and services) within the country and the region.

By third-world standards, we have a good human resource base. The large improvement to be made in the medium term is in tertiary, technical and vocational education.

There are several things in our favour.

- We are not abysmally poor by third-world standards but rather lower-middle income countries. The unequal distribution of income and significant poverty

and unemployment in many of our countries have been caused by years of economic contraction under internally chosen or externally imposed policies of economic stabilisation and structural adjustment.
- The population is almost completely literate and enjoys better education and health than in most developing countries, with capacity for training in skills both formally and on the job.
- We are well-placed geographically, at the centre of the three Americas (North, South and Central), and accessible through modern transport technology to western Europe. We could become a centre of production, trade and investment in the western hemisphere;
- There is a reasonably good natural resource base in the region.
- We are in a good position to increase our levels of savings and productive investment in the public, private and household sectors.
- In spite of the specific problems of some countries, there is the capacity to institute and continue with good macroeconomic management;
- We can generate locally and regionally more production of goods and services linked to the tourism industry, which would entail greater diversification of production and export patterns.
- There is the potential for developing services other than tourism which are "tradeable", that is, capable of earning foreign exchange.
- We can develop niche markets abroad in certain specialist 'high-quality' and unmistakably CARICOM or West Indian products.
- We have the capacity to attract both direct and portfolio foreign investment.

In order to become competitive in exports, increases in productivity, chiefly a combination of skills, better equipment, hard work and an eye for what would sell in foreign markets in all sectors and at all levels of the economies are essential. The neoclassical method of either continuing devaluation or free floating of the currency as an instrument for becoming more competitive is risky, since it can for a number of complicated and "expectational" psychological reasons get out of hand, although reasonable, if fairly small, devaluations may be made from time to time.

STABILISATION, STRUCTURAL ADJUSTMENT OR DEVELOPMENT POLICY?

The West Indies needs to stabilise the economies by achieving and maintaining both internal and external macroeconomic balance. Without stabilisation there can be no self-sustaining development – only "stop-and-go" development. Prolonged fiscal deficits are the chief cause of the lack of macroeconomic stability in our economies. These should be tackled at a very early stage, because otherwise the small open economies in the West Indies will continue to face inflation and balance-of-payments problems. The IMF is undoubtedly correct in its emphasis on the need for speedy action to eliminate fiscal deficits.

The term structural adjustment can be misleading; it can simply be a euphemism for a particular set of long-term development policies and strategies. A distinction should be made between stabilisation and development policy.

THE MEANING OF DEVELOPMENT

Growth and structural transformation are a necessary but not a sufficient condition for economic development.

First of all, the development process needs to be "endogenous" or "internalised" irrespective of the size or natural resources of the country; that is to say, domestic entrepreneurs (big, medium and small) should be flexible, innovative and risk-taking. In addition, development must come from both the top and below.

Widespread poverty, unemployment and inadequate human resources development must be alleviated and this is both a condition of further economic growth and development and an end in itself, because it develops the potential of people and their standard of living. Ultimately economic development is about the development of people. Certainly in the West Indies economic growth must be combined with equality, a view put by Nancy Birdsall, executive vice-president of IDB, in "Economic Development is Social Development".

Arthur Lewis's pioneering work, *The Theory of Economic Growth*, dealt with these factors. Recently the prime minister of Jamaica, P.J. Patterson, has appointed a task force to look at some aspects of this subject with the emphasis on the reduction of violence and crime.

DEVELOPMENT POLICIES FOR THE WEST INDIES

Arthur Lewis's presidential statement to the 1972 meeting of the board of governors of CDB is our point of departure here. The statement had no specific title, but it shows great insight into the requirements and appropriate policies for West Indian development. Lewis's theory was that we need to act on four elements to promote West Indian development:
- trade policy;
- exchange rate policy;
- incomes policy; and
- much higher productivity.

We have added a fifth important issue: sectoral policies and programmes.

Nothing can be done about import policy in the present neo-liberal global economy, except to produce more food for national, regional and extra-regional markets. In the bigger countries quantitative restrictions on imports have been abolished and a low CET has been accepted by all. On export policy, the state and the private sector can jointly achieve much by way of export promotion support and incentives.

Lewis gave great importance to devaluation as a means of making our economies more internationally competitive. From time to time it may be necessary to make small devaluations but too many and too frequent ones will create expectations of further devaluations, which could become self-fulfilling prophecies. Frequent devaluations bring about chronic inflation in small open developing economies and often may not be as effective in stimulating exports as in larger and more developed countries. Thus other instruments for promoting exports are needed, such as market information, research and development, quality standards and export credits. There was indeed much merit in the former currency board systems.

Incomes and prices policies are difficult for obvious social and political reasons. It may be possible for governments, the private sector and the trade unions to agree on broad guidelines concerning economically unjustified increases in money wages and salaries for a period of two or three years. The central technical issue here is whether there should be across-the-board national productivity guidelines for all sectors of the economy or whether increases in wage and salary levels could vary from enterprise to enterprise according to the increase in productivity over the last two or three years. (There is another problem about measuring productivity in service, as against goods-producing enterprises.) Barbados has started on this policy and their main social partners, the government, the trade unions and the private sector have recently signed a protocol on the implementation of incomes and prices policy. Jamaica has also begun negotiations with the social partners on wages, prices and incomes.

Lewis considered that enhancing productivity consisted not only of the efforts of managers and workers in the factory, farm and the office, but also of increasing the number of people with technical, para-professional or vocational skills and a really good secondary education. (We wish to enter a reservation here concerning the West Indies'-wide problem of a "mismatch" between the values and attitudes engendered in secondary schools and by parents with the job opportunities actually available in the economies). Manufacturing enterprises should improve and modernise equipment and plan new enterprises and establishments with plant and machinery geared to produce more goods for the growing demand abroad.

Greater Domestic Savings

Lewis stressed strongly the need for greater domestic savings in the private, household and public sectors, in all the CARICOM member states, encouraged by incentive schemes and the establishment and modification of relevant institutions.

DEVELOPMENT AND HIGH-TECH ACTIVITIES

The West Indies cannot hope within a few years to become a major producer and exporter of high-tech goods and services and move away from agricultural and manufactured products. To do this our educational and training systems would need substantial modification even in the medium term. The work should be initiated now so that significant results may be seen in around ten years.

Action should be undertaken urgently by the CARICOM region, since informatics and telecommunications are essential components of development as follows.

- The infrastructure for economic activity, gaining access to and expanding markets globally; providing commercial services to companies conducting just-in-time operations.
- The infrastructure for intra-regional networks, providing the medium for an information structure, the interchange of information to enhance the regional integration movement, carrying out commercial transactions within the single market, networking the regional trading organisations, commercial enterprises and public-sector organisations.
- The facilitating mechanism for providing regional and global services such as banking and insurance, tourism, entertainment and data entry.
- The infrastructure for carrying multimedia, creating opportunities through distance teaching, minimising travel expenditure through teleconferencing, creating informational and cultural products and services.

The region should form a plan of action to develop the information infrastructure in general and telecommunications in particular.[3]

MARGINALISATION, ABSORPTION OR INTERDEPENDENCE?

There is a danger that if the West Indies fails to become more self-reliant and more internationally competitive, by not following appropriate national and regional policies, it will become either marginalised or absorbed.

Marginalisation means economic stagnation with rising levels of unemployment and poverty, a failure to develop the levels and structures of skills or to increase production for national, regional and world markets sufficiently. At the same time a few at the top would be earning large incomes and those in the middle barely satisfactory ones. More people would therefore become economically and socially marginalised, making for a troublesome social situation. CARICOM would become useless and most likely fade away. Externally, the international community would regard us as of very little importance, except possibly as targets for humanitarian relief. Thus we would become marginalised both internally and externally.

The alternative is absorption (not necessarily *de jure* but certainly *de facto*). This means that we would become for all practical purposes absorbed into a powerfi country or group of such countries, probably individually and not as a group. (Remember the adage of the Roman Empire: "Divide and rule.") CARICOM would become irrelevant and die. A higher standard of living than under the marginalisation scenario for the better-off groups and for some of the middle-income groups might be feasible but unemployment would remain a serious problem. Much of our national and West Indian cultural identity would be eroded, leaving little real "sovereignty". Last and not least, we would have scarce self-respect and the rest of the world would ignore us and regard us with contempt.

There is a third scenario: let us call it interdependence or partnership between the West Indies, the rest of the Caribbean archipelago, the mainland countries, North America and Europe. This objective should find favour among thinking West Indians. The concept means earning our own way in the world rather than being dependent and mendicant, but very great efforts are required both at the national and regional levels to achieve this state of affairs.

INWARD- AND OUTWARD-LOOKING
DEVELOPMENT STRATEGIES

Is integration an inward-looking or an outward-looking process?

The terms "inward-looking" and "outward-looking" may be applied to certain patterns of development; inward-looking refers to national and regional import substitution, outward-looking to exporting to extra-regional markets. The simplest measure of either is the ratio of imports or exports to gross domestic product (GDP). A high dependence on foreign trade is regarded as outward-looking, and not surprisingly, small countries tend to fall into this category. This is so for two reasons.

In a small country nearly every economic activity – production, consumption and investment (in the sense of capital formation) – has a high import content, largely because its natural resource base tends to be much narrower than in a large country. Greater self-sufficiency is more attainable in a large country. High dependence on imports means that the country must earn large amounts of foreign exchange by exporting goods and tradeable services, so that it can meet its import bill. In the West Indies the present very high ratio of imported food and animal feeds to GDP cannot be excused on the grounds of small size, since both unutilised land and labour exist to make agricultural expansion feasible.

Second, economies of scale are more difficult to achieve for smaller countries because of the limited size of their domestic markets compared with larger countries. This means a heavy reliance on exports of manufactures and services.

For these two reasons small countries have no choice but to depend heavily on imports and on exports of goods and services to provide the foreign exchange to pay for their imports. The situation is worse when small countries have a high external debt service burden and are unnecessarily dependent on imported food.

Even when a group of small countries such as CARICOM forms an integrated group, a high ratio of extra-regional trade to GDP will still operate. Thus, even when an integrated group is formed, the external orientation of the group as a whole has to be outward-looking rather than inward-looking (except in a few activities such as the production of food, agro-industries and animal feeds).[4]

Ultimately all economic development, whether of individual countries or groups of countries (irrespective of size), must be inward-looking in the sense of being self-reliant, internationally competitive, flexible, resilient and quick to innovate or to shift resources to other activities. (Development ultimately "comes from within", to use the words of Oswaldo Sunkel, a former ECLAC economist.) This is a semantic but fundamental point. Singapore, for example, is by this criterion more inward-looking and more self-reliant than many larger third-world countries with a much lower ratio of foreign trade to GDP.

HUMAN CAPITAL AND SOCIAL CAPITAL

Everyone now accepts the vital role that human capital (resulting from programmes of human resource development) has to play in promoting sustained economic growth and development. A newer and quite distinct concept has recently been introduced into the development dialogue: social capital.

Social capital includes all the elements that make for a harmonious and cohesive society, one where there is great mutual trust between individuals and certain widely shared (even though unwritten) norms of conduct such as keeping one's word and meeting one's obligations, in other words a solidarity, individual trustworthiness, the formation of voluntary associations for achieving joint goals, and strong social discipline.

The extent of these characteristics varies even in developed democratic countries. For example, in the UK and North America the influence of individualism, of the ideas of John Locke, the seventeenth-century English moral and political philosopher is still strong. On the other hand, the economies of democratic developed countries such as Japan, Singapore, Germany, the Netherlands and the Scandinavian countries are based on social discipline, solidarity, cohesiveness and mutual trust in individuals and the community. The concept of social capital is particularly relevant in the contexts of a social partnership for an income and prices policy, short- and medium-term macroeconomic policies and longer-term development strategies.

The idea has been taken up by a few West Indian economists, mainly Brewster (who has applied it in a comparative study of Barbados and Jamaica), Clive Thomas and Mark Figueroa (See List of References).

TOWARDS AN EFFICIENT ECONOMY AND A JUST SOCIETY

The above discussion of West Indian development problems indicates that the overriding goal should be the creation of an efficient economy and a just society.

The most powerful framework for achieving efficient growth and structural change in an economy[5] is free, moderately state-controlled capitalism, led by entrepreneurs and managers of great energy and innovativeness and by an educated, highly trained and disciplined workforce. In particular, experience (rather than ideology or economic theory) has shown that a private sector, free-market economy is more capable of growth in export earnings than other forms of economic activity. But this form of economy also has shortcomings, principally because it can cause unemployment and poverty.

Some Considerations

1. Too extreme or rapid liberalisation of the economy, whether of protected local grown agricultural and manufactured products or of capital movements (particularly of "hot money flows" – as the recent experience of Mexico, Venezuela and Argentina shows) can be very dangerous for developing countries. The same may also apply to excessive and over-rapid deregulation of the financial sector.
2. The privatisation and divestment of state-owned enterprises and public utilities should be accompanied by state retention of minority equity and the offer of shares to employees.
3. Deregulation of prices and other controls or subsidies on the free market must be accompanied by legislation and machinery for supervising prices and rates. In the USA, for example, the rates, fares and prices of privately-owned public utilities and the operations of commercial banks, financial institutions and the stock markets are all highly regulated.
4. Private enterprises of all sizes must be encouraged by the state to become more efficient and internationally competitive. At the same time, the economy and the wider society cannot be left to be completely run by private enterprise and the free market or to be dominated by the extreme application of economic liberalisation policies. Some balance, good judgement and common sense must be exercised by the social partners.
5. There is no magic of the marketplace. There are technical deficiencies in the free play of market forces, such as: external economies; indivisibilities; monop-

oly and monopsony in both product and factor markets; the need for the state to provide public goods (e.g. education, health and infrastructure) the adverse impact upon the environment; lack of information on prices, alternative equipment and technology, failure in some cases of relative market prices to reflect relative scarcities and social cost of goods, services and factors of production.

Conclusion

State-encouraged and regulated capitalist enterprises of all sizes must play a major role in all our economies and the market must be given an important but by no means exclusive role. A less tidy arrangement might involve an active private sector (both local and foreign), a free market that works well in practice, together with the state, all managing macroeconomic and development policies and promoting anti-poverty and employment-generated programmes. Larger participation in the ownership and management of enterprise and in national economic and social decision-making by the social partners and by other groups in both urban and rural areas is necessary. All of these are needed to bring about efficient, internationally competitive economies and social justice in the West Indian countries. It is our profound conviction that a kind of purposeful, semi-visionary and yet pragmatic and concrete approach to the challenges of our economies and society is essential. Let us resolve to cast away the imported ideological slogans of the right, the left and indeed the centre. Let us develop and implement a 'West Indian approach.[6] A different orientation for the trade unions who should in any national or regional chapter of civil rights or Bill of Rights, include not only the rights of citizens and residents, but also the duties and obligations of every individual and group to the society and to the state.

Recommendations

1. Efficient internationally competitive economic growth and structural change must be a prime policy goal, since in developing countries this is a necessary (though not sufficient) condition of social justice.
2. Free market and private enterprise must be given wide, but not unfettered, scope.
3. The state must encourage and facilitate the private sector particularly in respect of exporting goods and services and promoting efficient production for the home and regional markets.
4. More broadly, the state must intervene sometimes: giving incentives (particularly to foreign exchange-earning activities); providing some special tariff protection and cheap credit; operating national standards organisations to set standards for exports and imports and assistance to local firms; imposing

countervailing duties and other barriers to prevent non-CARICOM countries exporting to us damaged or subsidised or dumped products (agricultural or manufactured).
5. The state must intensify its efforts to improve public-sector efficiency.
6. Extreme and rapid liberalisation of imports of locally and regionally produced products must be avoided as much as possible. Liberalisation of capital movements (particularly "hot money" inflows) and outflows must be avoided.
7. The state should work with the national, regional and extra-regional private sectors to promote production aimed primarily at the extra-regional export market.
8. The state must not deter productivity in the medium-size and large-scale private sector. It must also encourage both the establishment and the expansion of small-scale enterprises including self-employment.
9. The state should encourage the establishment of human resources development programmes in education training, agricultural technology and manufacture.
10. Informatics and telecommunications should be promoted by the state as well as the organised local and regional private sector through programmes of general education and specialised training which will have their results in the medium and long term.
11. The state should draw up well-targeted programmes to reduce unemployment and poverty. During periods of severe stabilisation adjustment programmes, it must set up a safety-net for the poor and the under-privileged. This is an important aspect of social justice.
12. In order to promote internationally competitive economic growth combined with social justice, prices and incomes policies within the framework of social partnership in all CARICOM countries must be introduced as a matter of urgency.
13. The state may have to be involved in joint ventures with local, regional and foreign private firms for minerals extraction, telecommunications and public utilities. In cases of divestment the employees must be offered shares in the enterprise. Some may view a "management contract" with an extra-regional firm as an alternative to divestment. The danger here is that the firm undertaking the management will not be facing any risk, so management contracts should always be combined with some ownership of shares by the management firm.
14. When public utilities are being privatised, the state should establish regulatory commissions with teeth. A fair trading commission is also required to keep price movements of basic commodities under surveillance, particularly when price controls and subsidies have been lifted.

15. The state should work alongside the local and regional private sectors and academia and support the adaptation of imported technology and local and regional research and development activities. But targets here must be realistic. We cannot become high-tech societies overnight.
16. The state and the Central Bank should always move quickly to regain macroeconomic stability as soon as the economic data indicate danger signals. But this is not a once-for-all objective. Stabilisation must be continuously sought in specific reaction to external and internal "shocks". If the stabilisation measures are too timid or not quick enough, traumatic and socially destabilising measures may have to be taken later.
17. Over time both macroeconomic and national and sectoral development policies and programmes in industry, agriculture, tourism and non-tourism services must be harmonised, as far as feasible, in the context of the creation of a CARICOM single market and economic union. The industrial policy proposals now being discussed in parliament in Jamaica could serve as a useful basis for other CARICOM countries, *mutatis mutandis*.
18. Economic growth and development must protect, and restore the environment.
19. Economic development in the context of greater self-reliance must come internally from both above and below and externally from diversified patterns of extra-regional exports of goods and services.
20. The social partners should vigorously seek to increase domestic savings by the public sector, the private sector and the household (or personal) sector.
21. There must be widespread participation in economic activities and in national decision-making based on the principle of social partnership.
22. Trade unions should pay more attention to: the stabilisation of employment levels within the enterprises of their membership; employment generation in other enterprises and sectors; and concentration on securing higher wages and other benefits from the enterprises in which their members are employed.
23. A rounded view of social justice calls not only for the satisfaction of economic and social rights of individuals and groups within the country but also for the proper discharge of obligation to society and to the state. This must be explicitly spelt out in any national or regional charters of social rights, which should be termed charters of social rights and obligations.

CONCLUDING OBSERVATIONS ON FISCAL POLICY

The major weakness in the economic policies of West Indian governments is fiscal, including both revenue and expenditure. There are other weaknesses, particularly in the monetary and exchange rate areas. The weakness is not lack of technical capacity but stems from "softness" towards the population and lack of political courage in the context of electoral solutions.

Development aid to the CARICOM countries has started to decline and will continue to do so. This means that in future the classical principle of a budget surplus will gain renewed importance. Thus political courage requires that within two years every West Indian country should have a surplus of recurrent revenue over recurrent expenditure (including debt amortisation) sufficient to finance at least one-third of capital expenditure. The rest will have to come from bilateral and multilateral aid, and from loans raised on local and regional capital markets with the residential covering markets.

If development aid is to be successfully sought, the country must make, and be seen to be making, the necessary fiscal effort and to be improving its tax assessment and collection machinery so that a much greater amount of the taxes levied would in fact be paid by the taxpayers.

The political decision-makers and their civil service advisers are not to blame. It is well known that wages and salaries make up a considerable portion of the recurrent expenditure of the central and local governments – some 40 - 2. Therefore the moderation of wages and salaries claimed by the trade unions representing public workers is essential to moderate total recurrent expenditure increases. Surely it is more important for public workers at all levels to maintain their jobs than to secure increases in pay well beyond the capacity of the government and the economy to pay.

In terms of economic efficiency and social justice, the tax and expenditure structure must promote both international competitiveness and the well-being of the poorest. Public-sector employees (both salary and wage earners) are not usually among the poorest and most deprived in the society. In countries where people living below the poverty line amount to 40 percent of the population, the claims of employees of the large and medium-sized private firms and of public-sector employees must be balanced against the claims of the truly poor.

NOTES

1. This paper does not deal with the by now well recognised issue of sustainable development, which is concerned with the impact of human activity on the environment. The essential feature of the environmental approach is that in all our economic activities we must not adversely affect the environment and, if possible, we must improve it. Writers on development should use precise terminology. The term sustainable development refers to development without environmental damage. The term self-sustaining growth and development is used to refer to continuing growth and development without regard to environmental effects. In this paper we cannot cover all aspects of West Indian development. Readers may refer to a recent

paper by Professor Bishnodat Persaud, 'Sustainable Development in the Caribbean' (UWI Centre of Environmental Studies, 1994).
2. The material on the quality of life in the West Indies and other developing countries are based on statistical and other reports of the CDB, World Bank, UNDP and UNICEF.
3. The substance of this last paragraph was suggested by Carol Collins, director of information and telecommunications of the CARICOM Secretariat.
4. For more on the small and very small country issue, see the work of Dennis Dean, Trevor Farrell and Paul Sweeten referred to in the List of References.
5. A brief and commonsense definition of modern capitalism in a system of production, distribution and exchange of goods and services, based largely on the free market and led by private enterprise, with varying degrees of state ownership, control and intervention.
6. We have not had the time nor the specific knowledge to make proposals for organising productive employment and foreign exchange earning activities at the level of the steelband, the reggae band the carnival band or other forms of West Indian cultural expression.

2

The Need for a Transition to Greater Self-Reliance and International Competitiveness

We have to become more self-reliant, resilient and internationally competitive so that we can become genuinely interdependent with the rest of the world over a reasonable period of time – say 10 -20 years. Of course, we will reach this position earlier in certain sectors and activities than in others and the transition periods will also vary from one area to another.

What Arthur Lewis wrote in his pioneering work on development economics, The Theory of Economic Growth, in 1955, about the importance of attitudes and the will to develop in economic development, still holds. Changes take time, as do changes in the systems of education and training; the results of research and development; the establishment or reform of institutions; the necessary changes in attitudes towards risk-taking; and doing new things or existing things in a new way. It also takes time to develop competitive strength in both goods and services.

Consider the preferences which we get for our exports of goods (particularly bananas and sugar in the EU and sugar in the USA) and from exports of agro-industrial and manufacturing products in the EU (under the Lomé Convention), in the USA (under the CBI) and in Canada (under CARIBCAN). The fact is that for the most part we do not produce at a unit cost which would make many of our products competitive at world prices.

The economies of the West Indies, although deriving benefits from natural resources in petroleum, bauxite, export-oriented agriculture and tourism, have not internalised the processes of growth and development. This is perhaps why our manufacturers have not taken much advantage of duty-free access to markets in western Europe and North America. However, quite a few manufacturers in one of the more developed countries (MDCs) of CARICOM are making a successful export drive to the duty-free markets of Venezuela and Colombia in the case of one and to the U.S. market in the case of the other.

Our argument is quite simple. It will be difficult for the CARICOM countries to move to reasonable self-reliance and international competitiveness within a short period of time. It is an exaggeration to label us "infant economies", since our highly export-led economies were created by European colonists centuries ago. A more accurate description would be "adolescent" economies suffering in many ways from arrested development. It will obviously take time for the adolescent to grow up to young adulthood and live outside the shelter of his parents' home.

But one fundamental problem remains – time. We have a good basis from which to start, but changes in attitude are a time-consuming process. It cannot be brought about by pulling a switch or pressing a push-button. If this is accepted, we still come up against the critical issue of how long it will take to change the attitudes and institutional bases of our economies and make us more competitive. For far too long, because of our economic and political history over the last 350 years our economies were protected by preferences for our exports and were unable to develop the entrepreneurial, managerial and technical skills to produce competitively in manufacturing and tradeable services other than tourism, which is a natural resource-based activity.

The West Indies must make very big efforts to move with speed to develop from adolescent to adult or at least near-adult status. No realistic West Indian can doubt this. The fundamental question is how quickly can this be done.

There was no question that the West Indies had to reduce rates of protective import duties and eliminate quantitative restrictions for local manufactures. This has been done (or is in the process of being done) in record time, but it still remains to be seen how quickly exports of manufactures will expand because of this tilt of the balance of incentives towards export orientation and away from highly protected national and regional import substitution. The magnitude of the problem would increase if in the medium term association with NAFTA/FTAA and the EU required full reciprocity (that is, total duty-free treatment for all imports from these two giant blocs). The problem also arises (to a somewhat lesser extent) where we have free trade agreements with countries such as Colombia and Venezuela. Here, immediate full reciprocity cannot be entertained, particularly with the OECS countries and Belize.

There are some ominous sounds emanating from some regional manufacturers that the greatly reduced level of protection, will force them either to go back to importing or go out of business entirely. An overdose of the best medicine may kill the patient! In many CARICOM countries there has been such a big reduction in protection (both tariffs and quantitative restrictions) that even on strictly economic grounds it is difficult to justify the granting of full tariff reciprocity by CARICOM to imports from larger countries or trading blocs. We have already conceded far too much, far too quickly, by way of trade liberalisation.

The process of the development of our human resources (professional, para-professional, technical and vocational) will have to continue. The question really is how soon can trained human resources be developed. Productivity in both the export and import-substitution sectors will have to rise significantly if we are to be internationally competitive in other than labour-intensive types of manufacturing industries. We have to concentrate on providing skilled and semi-skilled jobs.

If development aid is substantially diminished, it will make it difficult for both the LDCs and the MDCs to improve and maintain their physical infrastructure, upgrade human resources and strengthen the balance of payments (in so far as foreign aid covers a large part of the local cost element in projects being financed). The World Bank has already decided to terminate very soft International Development Association, (IDA) loans to the OECS countries of CARICOM. Instead, a mixture of hard and soft loans will be made to these countries. On the other hand, the IDB now intends to make available a fairly high amount of soft funds through CDB to the OECS countries.

Direct and portfolio foreign investment is largely in our hands. When the local and regional private sectors are seen to be investing in the production of goods and tradeable services, this will encourage direct investment from extra-regional sources. This attitude is also likely to induce venture capital funds to invest in our countries. The first one of these regional venture-capital funds is about to be established for the whole of CARICOM, and others may well be established in the future.

National and regional efforts, through both the deepening and widening of a more export-oriented CARICOM, can together be of great assistance in the accelerated structural transformation of West Indian economies. But the LDCs and the MDCs need to be allowed transitional periods.

It might be useful if a high-level group of technocrats from bodies such as the CARICOM Secretariat, the OECS Secretariat, CDB, the central banks, UWI and the University of Guyana, and from planning ministries and agencies, could meet to examine the issue of transition.

Continuing favourable preferential and non-reciprocal trading and financial and technological dependence on developed countries seems to be contrary to the idea of self-reliance. This is not really so; an appropriate philosophy of development for the Caribbean is "help towards self-help", to quote from an October 1994 statement by the European Union on development policy for Latin American and Caribbean countries.

After this chapter had been written, two World Bank documents were received. One was entitled *Caribbean Region: Strengthening Private Sector Development (1994)*. The other was called *Economic Policies for Transition in the OECS (1994)*. Both were for the most part well documented and in many areas provided sensible advice, although it is not clear why the World Bank saw the need for transition in the OECS and did not equally emphasize this need in the case of the other CARICOM countries. Moreover the length of the transition to greater self-rebate period (some five years) seems inadequate in both cases. Finally the World Bank study advocates full economic union among the OECS states, but does not advocate this particularly strongly for the whole of CARICOM).

3

The Rationale of Integration and the Essentials of CARICOM

THE BASIC RATIONALE OF INTEGRATION AMONG DEVELOPING COUNTRIES

Economic integration involves in varying degrees the pooling of national markets as well as natural, financial and human resources. All of this creates greater economic space for each member of the integration grouping. To use a term borrowed from physics, integration and cooperation can help to achieve a critical mass in a group of small countries.

The pooling of markets and resources and the consequential creation of greater economic space is particularly necessary in small and very small countries such as those in CARICOM. The most populous country, Jamaica, is very small compared with other countries, with a population of 2.4 million. For the smaller countries of CARICOM (with an average population of about 100,000 each), the formation of a CARICOM single market of just under 6 million persons represents a crucial widening of opportunities and mutual benefits.

Trade and production are not the only areas in which national economies can be brought together, resulting in enhanced cost-effectiveness. Examples are common services in tertiary education (UWI); secondary school examinations (Caribbean Examinations Council, CXC); health; sea and air transport; some aspects of defence and security; development banks and financial institutions (such as the Caribbean Development Bank); the Caribbean Food Corporation (CFC) and the Caribbean Research and Development Institute (CARDI); anti-drug surveillance; anti-pollution activities to protect the sea and other parts of the environment; fisheries and fishing grounds. The trained and specialised personnel in most fields are so few in number that we have to make use of them in region-wide institutions or in regional pools of experts. The OECS is one of the few groups in the world today with a single multinational central bank.

There are many non-governmental common services which have worked well and have helped to promote the West Indies throughout the world; the West Indian cricket team, CANA, CBU, the Caribbean Congress of Labour, the Caribbean Association of Industry and Commerce (CAIC), the Caribbean Conference of Churches and other non-governmental regional bodies (including women and youth groups).

Functional cooperation is possible without common services. Its value lies in exchanging experiences with common problems and their solutions can help individual member states to learn from each other. Of notable importance in functional cooperation are the Caribbean Festival of Arts (CARIFESTA) and the group whose concern is measures to raise the status of women in the West Indies, CAFRA.

Integration, in so far as it extends to a common external tariff CET policy and the coordination of external trade, foreign policy and joint negotiations on matters of common interest, can increase the external bargaining power of a group of small countries.

However, the instruments of integration can be used not merely to promote efficient national and regional import substitution and positively facilitate and push production of exports to extra-regional markets. CARICOM can play a most helpful part in West Indian development.

We must be intellectually honest and put forward here the case against the purely economic aspects of integration groupings of developing countries, both big and small.

It is argued by neo-classical and by neo-liberal economists that an integration grouping can lead to trade diversion, that is, the switch from previously imported goods from third countries (at reasonably low prices) to importing more costly products from other members of the group. This causes a loss of economic welfare; moreover, the costs of trade diversion fall more heavily on the less developed countries than on the more developed ones who have a more advanced industrial sector within the grouping, since in the first stages the latter carry out most of the existing and incremental industrial production.

See the Treaty of Chaguaramas establishing the Caribbean Community, CARICOM Secretariat, 1973.

The incompleteness of this approach has been pointed out over the years by many writers on development. We may reply by showing the need to take account of the following considerations, many of which have effects in the medium and long term.

- The greater the export orientation of the grouping, the lower the costs of trade diversion will be – this could be so if the CET and the level of quantitative

restrictions have been considerably lowered. This would result in lower prices for regionally produced goods. However, this argument cannot be pushed too far since very big reductions in protection might wipe out existing industries.
- Economies of scale and specialisation and external economies are likely to emerge over time, thus lowering unit costs of production.
- Employment creation within the region.
- The "infant industry" argument for protection in developing countries.
- Lower unit costs can be achieved in time by learning by doing.
- The fact that the pessimistic "trade diversion" view is based on "static" assumptions and does not take into account medium and longer-term "dynamic" aspects (or, as it is sometimes called, incremental comparative advantage).
- Both the neo-classical and neo-liberal theories assume that resources of land, labour and capital are all fully employed, which is by no means so in developing countries such as CARICOM member states.
- A whole range of special measures to prevent the lagging behind of the relatively less developed members.
- CDB, both in its charter and its operation, has always given priority to funding capital projects and technical assistance to the LDCs, especially with respect to the use of concessional or "soft" funds, even though the MDCs have contributed a much higher share of ordinary capital and soft resources of the bank than the LDCs.

We consider that efforts to achieve an optimum allocation of resources in the short run can cause errors when dealing with the effects of economic integration on both national and regional welfare and development.

A New but Dubious Argument about the Distribution of Benefits of Trade Liberalisation and Integration Among Unequal Partners

A new argument has been advanced that in reciprocal free trade between a very big and a very small country all the gains accrue to the very small country and all the losses to the very big country. In support of this proposition is the fact that foreign trade is much more important to a small country (which has to specialise) than to a larger more developed country which is less dependent on foreign trade, most of its production being sold on the domestic market.

This argument is different from both the classical and neo-classical theories of comparative advantage and newer theories such as the competition advantage of nations. It also runs contrary to the "publication" argument of development economists such as Gunnar and to the unequal exchange arguments of Lewis and Prebisch. The argument has, in fact, no foundation in practice. It is well known that trade liberalisation, deeper economic integration or political union lead to more losses for the smaller less developed countries than for the bigger more developed ones.

The argument would be more accurate if the countries were at similar levels of economic and social development in terms of high income per head, the use of advanced technologies and a diversified, resilient and flexible structure in the pattern of production and exports. The economies of CARICOM, the Caribbean archipelago and the Central American countries do not exhibit these characteristics.

All free trade areas, deeper forms of integration and nation-states with wide disparities in levels of development as between different parts of the region or the country – even with free movement of labour and/or capital – pursue a wide range of non-reciprocal and anti-polarisation measures – including non-reciprocity by the less developed parties. This is true of the Generalised System of Preferences (GSP), the CBI, CARIBCAN, the EU, CARICOM, the Andean Group and the Central American Common Market (CACM). It is also true of states such as the USA, Canada, Italy, the UK, Germany and France.

NEW THRUST IN REGIONAL INTEGRATION

The aim of the type of common market integration which we have been discussing is regional import substitution. But if the CARICOM Treaty can be revised so as to permit a positive effect on extra-regional exports, we are in a new ball-game. Even the present unrevised CARICOM treaty in Article 46 of the Common Market Annex makes specific provision for the promotion of manufactured exports outside CARICOM. A revised treaty should provide for more export-oriented development and integration.

Successful promotion of both goods and services to extra-regional markets will increase real income and purchasing power in the CARICOM countries and will result in more efficient national and regional import substitution.

Towards Open Regionalism

The worldwide trend today is towards open regionalism, to use the phrase coined by ECLAC. This approach to regional integration does not oppose all types of national and regional import substitution but calls for efficient national and regional import substitution by avoidance of excessively high protection which allows producers in such enterprises to earn excessive economic rents at the expense of consumers.

It would be difficult to establish a new industry on the basis that it will receive excessively rather than moderately high protection for a specified number of years;

for when the time comes for dismantling the excessive protection, political pressure can be brought to bear upon governments in order to preserve the jobs of those employed in such enterprises.

This has two policy implications: first, high protective barriers must begin to be phased out (but not eliminated in all cases) over a period of time; and second, the phasing-out should begin with a selective set of industrial activities. In other words a more gradualist and less comprehensive (across the board) treatment should be applied, with all new enterprises having to accept from the beginning moderate protection.

Levels of Intra-Regional Trade

The percentage of intra-regional trade in the total trade of the CARICOM member states has always been fairly small. The volume of imports by member states from CARICOM is about 8 percent of the imports from all countries, although the percentage varies from country to country, with the LDCs and Barbados having a higher percentage than most of the MDCs. The following points are relevant.

- The visible exports from CARICOM countries to the outside world are dominated by natural resource-based activities – oil, bauxite and alumina, fertilisers, sugar and bananas – and the major market for these exports is the developed countries of the world.
- Manufactures are not yet predominant in the exports of the CARICOM countries.
- The countries are small and, as explained earlier, have to depend on imports from other countries (mainly, but by no means only, the developed ones).
- If we can export much more manufactures, agro-industrial and non-traditional agricultural products, there will be two effects. Some of these exports will go to CARICOM. Incomes per head will rise and, assuming much greater capacity for producing exports, some of the increased income will be spent on local and regional goods. Thus there is a paradox that CARICOM's success in exporting to extra-regional markets may lead to reasonably efficient regional import substitution which will increase the percentage of intra-regional trade.
- There is great scope for increased food production to go to both the national and CARICOM markets in many member states of CARICOM. Low levels of intra-regional trade in food are said to be due to deficiencies in organisation and marketing; attempts to increase intra-CARICOM agricultural trade must seek to overcome these problems.

In spite of the low amount of intra-regional trade, one member country has a high level of exports to the rest of CARICOM and is the largest supplier of intra-regional exports in respect of both total exports and manufactured exports. It also has the highest visible trade surplus in intra-CARICOM trade. This is an important part of the case for widening CARICOM and retaining free access to external markets in North America and Europe.

Integration and Discrimination against Third Countries

Discrimination against outsiders is practised by all regional blocs, sub-regional groups and individual states. Indeed, regional cooperation and integration (whether at the level of continental blocs or at the level of sub-regional groupings) may be defined as a constructive form of discrimination. This was fully accepted by the original GATT agreement and it was certainly not rejected by the Uruguay Round.

Any trade and economic integration grouping (whether among developed or developing countries), if it is to mean anything, must involve some element of discrimination against countries not in the grouping. Some examples of discrimination follow.

- Even a loose free-trade or preferential bloc discriminates against countries (developed and developing) not in the grouping, in terms of market access. Similarly, rules of origin discriminate against third countries.
- A common external tariff (CET) discriminates against third countries, and, under the old GATT, had to be no higher than the average of the pre-existing national tariffs.
- A regime of monetary integration, exchange rates, legal tender arrangements, convertibility, exchange controls and even the monitoring of inflows and outflows of payments for transactions, involves discrimination against third countries.
- An integrated capital and money market in a grouping discriminates against third countries.
- The rights of non-member countries of the grouping to establish businesses, to provide services, to be eligible for governmental procurement and to invest in economic enterprises must also entail discrimination against third countries.
- Freedom of movement of labour and of managerial, technical and other skills between the member states of a grouping entails discrimination against nationals of third countries.
- Special arrangements are always made to benefit the less developed countries as compared with the more developed. This is a form of double discrimination in favour of less developed countries.
- At the heart of the existence of the modern nation-state is the fact that citizens and sometimes permanent residents are usually in a better position than non-

citizens or non-permanent residents, for example in terms of access to public, low-income housing and scarce secondary school places at better secondary schools. (This suggests that complete globalisation of the world economy cannot be feasible without democratic world government.)

THE FOUNDATIONS OF CARICOM

CARICOM represents an attempt at closer cooperation, economic integration and foreign and external trade policy coordination on the part of the former colonies of the UK in the sub-region. They are all islands, with the three exceptions of Belize, Guyana and Suriname. The total population of the group stands at 6 million persons and the total land area is about 100,000 square miles. The physical area is taken up mainly by the two countries situated on the mainland, Guyana in South America (83,000 square miles) and Belize in Central America (12,000 square miles).

The areas in their territorial waters (extending 12 miles out) and in their Exclusive Economic Zones (extending 200 miles from their coastline) should also be included. To the extent that these marine resources prove valuable, they would be a most important addition to the region's resources.

In early 1958 ten of the islands, then UK colonies, formed – with strong encouragement from the UK – a political federation, but it lasted only four years (from 1958 to 1962). (For a review of the Federation, see John Mordecai's book, *The Federal Negotiation*; the author was the most senior civil servant in the Federal Government.) Between 1962 and 1978 all of them, with the exception of Montserrat, became politically independent. The Caribbean Free Trade Association (CARIFTA) was established in 1968. This was a very loose trade grouping which was upgraded after five years of its operation into the tighter CARICOM, brought into existence by the Treaty of Chaguaramas (4 July 1973).

CARICOM aimed at deepening the integration process started by CARIFTA whose agreement (in a special annex) contained some of the steps to be taken to deepen economic integration.

All the heads of government agreed in 1989 in the Grand Anse Declaration that CARICOM should move towards an economic union (a single market and economy) by the year 2000.

The Three Aspects of the Caribbean Community

CARICOM operates in three areas: economic integration, pursued through the common market; common services and functional cooperation; and the coordination of the foreign policies of member states.

The Caribbean Common Market

The common market provides for free intra-regional trade, for a CET, for consultation on national economic policies (including exchange-rate changes) and for coordinated efforts in areas such as agricultural and industrial development, joint development of natural resources and the harmonisation of fiscal incentives to industries.

Many within and outside the region have overlooked the achievements of CARICOM. When we consider the punishing economic and financial crises which most of the member countries have experienced over the last 17 or 18 years, it is a miracle that CARICOM's common market has survived. In that period the majority of third world sub-regional and regional integration groupings have disintegrated (like the East African Community) or become inactive without being formally dissolved (like ECOWAS, CACM and the Andean Group).

There have been many defects in the functioning of CARICOM for some time. This was fully recognised by the conference of heads of government when they issued the Grand Anse Declaration in Grenada in 1989 (see Appendix A).

Common Services and Functional Cooperation

CARICOM's common services and functional cooperation are in many non-economic fields, such as education, examinations, health, culture, sea and air transportation, information and broadcasting, and enhancing the role and status of women in Caribbean society. Successes in these areas include the University of the West Indies (UWI) which pre-dates the Federation; test cricket, a non-governmental activity which pre-dates even UWI; the establishment of the CXC, CANA, CBU and CARIFESTA. These are often played down, but they are essential. Common services, for example, reduce unit costs by achieving critical mass. Where there are no common services, there is extensive cross-fertilisation and useful exchanges of views and experiences, resulting often in common approaches which have been originally implemented by one or two member states.

Coordination of Foreign and External Trade Policies

The all-important coordination of foreign and external trade policies is essential for small, weak and vulnerable economies such as those of CARICOM, for we must always seek to maximise our bargaining power in external trading, economic and diplomatic affairs by common policies and joint actions. In the field of external trade policy the integrity of the Community (especially as regards the CET) must always be preserved.

THE GOVERNANCE OF THE COMMUNITY

In the governance of the Community there is no trace whatsoever of supra-nationality, which is absent from the Treaty of Chaguaramas, the Grand Anse Declaration, the Report of the West Indies Commission and the decisions of the heads of government. Decisions of the conference of heads of government, the council and the ministerial committees are made unanimously and it is left to each individual government to implement them. Clearly, if CARICOM is to achieve its goals, there must be more effectiveness in its governance, even if an instrument other than the one proposed by the West Indian Commission has to be adopted.

A WARNING: AN OBSERVATION ABOUT CARIBBEAN INTEGRATION

It would be pertinent to end this chapter with a warning. In no part of the world, including the developing world, does integration in itself bring advantages. Integration helps to provide a framework within which both the public and private sectors have to be active. It is merely a facilitating process. If the governments do not stabilise their economies, do not have a sound development policy and are unwilling to coordinate their external trade and other policies, there will be little concrete progress in the integration movement. If the private sector is not active in using the opportunities created by the framework, there will be no growth and diversification in production and exports. The economic agents must exploit all the opportunities created by the integration instruments.

OTHER CARIBBEAN COUNTRIES' DESIRE TO JOIN CARICOM

A very important development is that other countries want to join the community. Since 1973 Suriname had been trying to become a member, but consideration of the application had to be postponed for many years because of the political domination by the military of the civil affairs of that country since 1980. The political atmosphere has become more propitious and the conference of heads of government, held in July 4, 1995, made Suriname a member. Both Haiti and the Dominican Republic have also long been interested in joining the Community. CARICOM must have a very good reputation if neighbouring countries persist over so many years to become members.

THE LESS DEVELOPED COUNTRIES IN THE CARIBBEAN COMMUNITY

One of the central problems of all integration groupings (whether it is a loose free-trade area or a tightly-knit economic union, or whether it is a large grouping or a small one) is the tendency for the benefits to accrue to the more developed countries. This is true of the EU, NAFTA, the Andean Group, Mercosur and CARICOM. Therefore there have to be specific arrangements to ensure benefits for the LDCs, because if everything were left to market forces, they would retrogress. In economic jargon this syndrome is termed polarisation.

Thus any integration movement or loose trade association between countries at various levels of development must contain a special regime to enable the LDCs to share equitably in the benefits of the integration process.

The Treaty of Chaguaramas establishing CARICOM contains a whole special regime for the LDCs. See Chapter 4. The CDB, with a membership larger than CARICOM, is rightly regarded by the LDCs as an essential component of their participation in the Caribbean integration process.

The LDCs in CARICOM consist of the member states of the OECS island member states and Belize on the Central American mainland. For reasons of propinquity and their very small size, the OECS was formed among seven of the Leeward and Windward Islands (Antigua and Barbuda, St Kitts and Nevis, Montserrat, Dominica, Grenada, St Lucia and St Vincent and the Grenadines). The OECS was established under the Treaty of Basseterre of 1982. The organisation has made much progress since then in many aspects of economic cohesion in common services and functional cooperation and in the harmonisation (not merely coordination) of their foreign policies, including external trade and economic policies. In addition, the four heads of governments of the Windward Islands made the sensible decision to establish a political union among all the OECS member states. Although this has not yet been achieved, that objective remains the goal of most thinking people in the OECS countries. However, in the meantime, they can still make progress in economic integration, common services and functional cooperation, and in the harmonisation of their foreign policies.

John Compton, the former prime minister of St Lucia must be complimented for his fortitude and determination in 'staying the course'. An unflagging supporter of West Indian unity, he was not disheartened by the lack of success in recent efforts at political union among the Windward Islands and just before demitting office called for further steps to be taken to strengthen and deepen the OECS among all its member states (even if this entails Political Union), in a manner which would strengthen CARICOM.

OECS has had some success in managing its joint economies and fiscal affairs – in some cases, better than other CARICOM countries. A crucial contributory factor has been their multi-national central bank, the Eastern Caribbean Central Bank (ECCB), which restricts the scope for both devaluation and excessive lending to the individual governments. In other sectors of economic policy, however, there appears to be a tendency towards retrogression in a growing number of the OECS member states.

4

The Grand Anse Declaration and the Establishment of the West Indian Commission

THE GRAND ANSE DECLARATION ON ACHIEVING A SINGLE MARKET AND ECONOMY

By the late 1980s there was widespread feeling throughout the Region that CARICOM, as it operated in practice, was not living up to its full potential. The common market process seemed to have lost its impetus. Foreign policy coordination had been functioning reasonably well but more could have been achieved. The only one of the three areas of activity of CARICOM that functioned satisfactorily was that of common services and functional cooperation. This was in spite of the urgent and realistic recommendations to strengthen CARICOM by a Group of West Indies Experts (chaired by the writer) appointed by the CARICOM Council of Ministers and Standing Committee of Ministers of Foreign Affairs on the urging of Henry Forde, Minister of Foreign Affairs of Barbados at the time. The report of the group was aptly entitled *The Caribbean Community in the 1980s*.

A major problem existed in all areas of CARICOM activity: the failure of member states to implement the decisions made at all levels. This problem arose largely because the Treaty of Chaguaramas (1973) had avoided even the remotest suggestion of supra-nationality in community organs and institutions (unlike, say, the European Community, now EU). The CARICOM treaty explicitly states that community decisions are left to each member state to implement in accordance with its own constitutional, legal and administrative procedures.

CARICOM was given a new lease on life by the conference of heads of government, meeting in Grand Anse, Grenada, in 1989. There the heads of government took far-reaching decisions aimed at creating a single market and single economy (economic union) by the year 2000. They took many specific decisions such as the establishment of joint embassies abroad and a Caribbean Court of Appeal to replace the Judicial Committee of the Privy Council in London. They agreed on the speedy introduction of two regimes to promote national and regional development in manufacturing and other sectors: the CARICOM Enterprise Regime and the Caribbean Industrial Programming Scheme (CIPS).

In 1990, the heads of government took another decision on a proposal submitted by Erskine Sandiford, the then Prime Minister of Barbados, to deepen integration further by achieving monetary integration by the year 2000. They also agreed to set up a CARICOM assembly drawn from national parliaments, with purely deliberative (as against law-making) powers.

THE ESTABLISHMENT OF THE WEST INDIAN COMMISSION

At the meeting in Grand Anse, the heads of government considered a paper submitted by A.N.R. Robinson, the then prime minister of Trinidad and Tobago. This paper drew attention to the fact that the year 1992 would be the 500th anniversary of the arrival of Europeans in the New World and proposed that he and his colleagues should take the opportunity to review the West Indian past and to look forward to the West Indian future in the twenty-first century.

REPORT OF THE WEST INDIAN COMMISSION

It was decided to set up the West Indian Commission chaired by Shridath Ramphal, Chancellor of UWI. The Vice-Chancellor of UWI, Alister McIntyre, was the vice-chairman and the author was a member of the Commission. A.N.R. Robinson stated that the other heads of government were just as concerned with where the West Indian peoples and countries were heading on the five-hundredth anniversary of the arrival of Europeans in the hemisphere in 1492.

The terms of reference of the commission were very far-reaching.[1]

The commission reported in 1992. The heads of government accepted all their major recommendations except the one concerning the establishment of a permanent commission of eminent West Indians (including the CARICOM secretary-general) with experience at a high level in public policy and international affairs, to speed up the national implementation of the decisions made at meetings at the Community level. They were to be responsible for persuading the governments of the member states to implement community decisions.

Since then a further role for the Commission has clearly emerged: the initiation, negotiation and follow-up of trade and economic agreements with both Caribbean and non-Caribbean countries and trading blocs. The Commission would have no legal powers, but they would bring to bear in all their actions an expression of a Community (as distinct from a national) point of view. The call for a commission along these lines was certainly not intended to reduce the powers of governments of member states or usurp the important place of the CARICOM secretariat in the CARICOM movement. It was merely a small addition to the Community's institutional machinery, designed to overcome a major fundamental weakness of the community.

The heads of government rejected the proposal for a permanent commission and decided instead to set up a three-man heads of government bureau, together with the CARICOM secretary-general, to meet regularly on a rotating basis for the purpose of monitoring the implementation of Community decisions by the member states. However, the heavy workload involved in this process is not appropriate for heads of government, who are already overburdened. The members of the bureau should be the ministers responsible for CARICOM affairs, such as ministers of foreign affairs. There are already two heads of government meetings every year (the regular one during the first week of July and another inter-sessional one halfway between).

Here is a short list of the decisions made by the heads of government based in many cases on the recommendations of the Report of the West Indian Commission. All in all, the Report contained well over 100 recommendations, many of which will be considered in the next two years.

The commission fully endorsed most of the proposals in the Grand Anse Declaration and in some cases fleshed them out.

- Reaffirmation of the intention to establish a West Indian Court of Appeal to replace the Judicial Committee of the Privy Council.
- The formation of an assembly of CARICOM parliamentarians.
- The establishment of a CARICOM charter of civil society to help assure good governance and the promotion of human rights, properly integrated.
- A new and more complete Common External Tariff (CET) for goods imported from outside the common market should be adopted and implemented by all member countries.
- Intra-regional trade should be freed of all obstacles, both tariff and non-tariff.
- The Caribbean Community should continue as a grouping of independent sovereign states.
- The Treaty of Chaguaramas should be revised.
- There should be a minister for CARICOM affairs in all member states and there should be a wider role for the Council of Ministers, who would be responsible not only for the common market but for the other ministerial standing committee.
- Here is a short list of the decisions made by the heads of government based in many cases on the recommendations of the Report of the West Indian Com-

mission. All in all, the Report contained well over 100 recommendations, many of which will be considered in the next two years.

The establishment of the Association of Caribbean States (ACS), included not only CARICOM countries but also most of the other islands in the Caribbean archipelago as well as the mainland countries whose shores are washed by the Caribbean Sea. This was a major step in the pragmatic expansion of the process of economic and other cooperation in the wider Caribbean.

NOTE

1. *Time for Action*; see *Report of the West Indian Commission*, 1992.

5

Clarification of Some CARICOM Issues

NATURAL AND HUMAN RESOURCES OF THE WEST INDIES

Natural Resources

The quality of human resources determines the level of self-sustaining development of any country or member of an economic grouping. Yet we cannot ignore natural resources as a means of earning revenue and foreign exchange, which has traditionally not been fully understood in the region. The present nature of tourism in most of the CARICOM countries means that the great majority of people who visit us are attracted by the natural resources of the sun, sea and sand and the places of environmental interest. For instance, an important part of Antigua's natural resources consists of a very large number of quiet, peaceful bays and coves. In Belize there are the cays for sun, sand and sea tourism and also interesting environmental and archaeological features. Guyana has a rich array of eco-tourism features.

All the CARICOM countries have the natural resources of being well located geographically for the purpose of production, trade and investment, standing at the crossroads of North, Central and South America and not too far from western Europe, given modern transportation facilities.

In most of the CARICOM countries the land resources are well suited for various forms of agriculture, including livestock. However, irrespective of size and population, large areas of cultivable land and many people are unused or underutilised.

The region continues to squander scarce foreign exchange in importing food for human consumption and animal feeds. Belize, Guyana, Jamaica and Trinidad and Tobago have good beef and dairy livestock potential; Belize and Guyana both have rich and accessible fisheries and other seafood resources. Surely no decision-maker or planner can rationalize this situation on the grounds of "comparative advantage" – because the situation falls far short of full employment. Here, as is often the case, common sense is a better guide than economic theory. Again, much of our fisheries (both fish and other seafood) are exploited by other countries, using modern trawlers within our Exclusive Economic Zones and sometimes within our 12-mile territorial seas. On the other hand, Belize, Guyana and The Bahamas are exploiting their rich endowment for fish and other seafood.

The following resources should also be mentioned. The bauxite resources of Guyana and Jamaica. The petroleum and natural gas reserves of Trinidad and Tobago. The modest levels of crude oil and natural gas of Barbados. The potential oil and hydroelectric resources of Belize and Guyana. The gold mining and processing by modern factories in Guyana. The timber resources of Belize, Dominica, Guyana, Jamaica, St Vincent and the Grenadines and Trinidad and Tobago. The potential for making marble in Jamaica.

The Exclusive Economic Zones of the individual CARICOM countries should not be forgotten, since it is possible that on and below the sea-bed there are various forms of wealth which could make an important contribution to the economic well-being of the West Indian peoples.

Human Resources

Human resources are of fundamental importance in achieving economic growth and development.

From a cultural, intellectual, entertainment and sporting point of view, West Indians have made and continue to make a contribution to the world quite out of proportion to the region's small total population of just under 6 million people.

St Lucia, with a population of about 150,000, has in 14 years produced two winners of the Nobel Prize in subjects as disparate as economics and literature (the late Arthur Lewis and Derek Walcott, respectively). This stunning achievement must have raised the self-esteem of many West Indians and the fact that this has occurred in a country of 150,000 people (out of a total world population of 5.5 billion) is astonishing.

Our region has made a significant cultural impact on the rest of the world in the form of Jamaican reggae and the Trinidad and Tobago calypso and steelpan, the latter being the only new musical instrument to have been invented in the twentieth century as Edward Seaga, the then prime minister of Jamaica said during a CARICOM heads of government conference in July 1983. These musical innovations have come from the grass-roots people of our countries, like Bob Marley and Slinger Francisco (Sparrow).

Above all, the English gentleman's game of cricket has been taken over by West Indians who have transformed the originally staid game into a sport of speed, daring, verve and elegance. George Headley was obviously one of the greatest world batsmen. In the last 25 years two West Indians, Garfield Sobers and Brian Lara, have made the highest batting scores recorded in one innings in test cricket. Frank Worrell and Clive Lloyd have been amongst the greatest batsmen and captains. Viv Richards also will always occupy a prominent place among the list of the great batsmen.

Since the early 1940s our region, mainly Jamaica, has produced great track athletes, including women such as Merlene Ottey.

In both the pre- and post-independence years we have produced a number of important political and trade union leaders.

West Indian writers have made a strong contribution to the world's literature. C.L.R. James is considered a towering intellectual and creative figure of the twentieth century. Due acknowledgement has yet to be paid in the region to one of our most gifted sons in both creative and historical writing, literary criticism, political and social thought and in the assistance which he gave to the struggle for independence in Ghana and Kenya. Not least, he also wrote about cricket: his book, *Beyond A Boundary*, is a fine piece of literature, containing deep insights, not only into West Indian and world cricket, but into West Indian society and world civilisations. He was an outstanding Shakespearean scholar.

Eric Williams, in his erudite and lucidly elegant *Capitalism and Slavery*, established himself as a first-rate Caribbean political and economic historian of the twentieth century, before going on to become the senior researcher in the Caribbean Commission. His contribution to Trinidad and Tobago and West Indian historical and political analysis is undeniable.

Vidia Naipaul is widely regarded as amongst the best writers of English prose today. Other important creative writers are George Lamming, Kamau Brathwaite, Martin Carter, Wilson Harris, John Hearne and Andrew Salkey.

West Indians are good teachers both at home and in the diaspora. (An eminent UK economist, Lionel Robbins, described Arthur Lewis as "perhaps the greatest teacher the London School of Economics has produced".

Not to be forgotten is the large number of professionals in law, medicine, dentistry, natural and applied science, banking, nursing, accountancy, actuarial work, insurance, engineering, design and construction and computer sciences, who serve both at home and in the diaspora. Nor must we forget that a person born of West Indian (Jamaican) parentage in the diaspora, Colin Powell, rose to the highest rank in the US armed forces as Chairman of the Joint Chiefs of Staff.

We have produced people who have held, or who hold high office in international organisations such as the Commonwealth, UNDP, the Pan-American Health Organisation (PAHO), the Organisation of American States (OAS) and the Food and Agriculture Organisation (FAO) of the UN. We have also produced first-class public servants and diplomats. Our contribution to academia, both at home and in the diaspora, is also noteworthy.

There is also a large number of West Indian entrepreneurs and managers who run large-scale commercial, industrial, agricultural, tourism and financial enterprises.

It is clear that West Indian people have made and are making an impact in significant areas of human activity both at home and in the rest of the world. In spite of the size of the countries, centuries of political and economic colonialism, the dehumanisation of slavery and the degradation of indentureship, West Indians have always proved their worth.

We have to make use of our potential and learn to transform challenges into opportunities. We need people with directly work-related skills – medium-sized entrepreneurial, managerial, technical, vocational and productive skills, since our main weakness is in the field of practical economic activity at the level of both the enterprise and the individual. Why have so many of the groceries and supermarkets set up in the diaspora for selling West Indian food been more or less monopolised by non-West Indians? There seems to be an inability to innovate and to achieve economic diversification and international competitiveness. As UWI Vice-Chancellor Alister McIntyre has long pointed out education should enhance the capacity for problem solving.

There are exceptions to these generalisations, particularly in Guyana and Trinidad and Tobago and through the survival and entrepreneurial instincts shown by large numbers of small people (independent of ethnicity and particularly women) in the informal sector in Jamaica, Guyana and the Windward and Leeward Islands.

IS CARICOM TOO SMALL TO BE A BASIS FOR WEST INDIAN ECONOMIC TRANSFORMATION?

It is often asserted that a combined CARICOM would be too small an economic unit to make a substantial contribution to the process of West Indian economic transformation. But this argument does not hold.

The combined population is just under 6 million, so that the pooling of markets and resources through CARICOM must be more effective than going it alone. Nearly all the individual units have a population of less than 250,000 each with the exceptions of Barbados, Guyana, Jamaica and Trinidad and Tobago. A unified West Indies must be more effective than the sum of its parts.

Both CARIFTA and CARICOM were always conceived of as only an intermediate stage, so that its members could learn how to export; this would be a first learning step to prepare them for wider Caribbean and extra-regional markets. The leaders of the countries never saw integration as being limited to regional import substitution. There was no underlying concept of a literally economically self-sufficient CARICOM, except for a few romantics who believed that we could go back to a simple, unsophisticated life. But we cannot, for we have lost our innocence in this regard.

We must recognise the economic and social successes of other small countries like Switzerland (6.8 million), Hong Kong (5.8 million), Denmark (6.8 million people), Luxembourg (400,000), the Irish Republic (3 million), Singapore (2.8 million) and New Zealand (3.5 million).

We are now engaged in widening CARICOM so that we can have a Caribbean Community co-extensive with the entire Caribbean archipelago of some 32 million people. If the idea of a Free-Trade Area of the Americas (FTAA) materialises, we will become part of the biggest trade bloc in the world, while we preserve our identity through a widened and closely integrated Caribbean Community.

To conclude this section, we quote from the October 1993 UWI graduation address at the Mona Campus delivered by Dennis Lalor, an outstanding figure of the Jamaican private sector with a clear West Indian vision:

> CARICOM with a population of 6 million people living on a land mass of 120,000 square miles, including Belize and Guyana, larger than the United Kingdom whose population is 57 million, is regarded internationally as a region which lives off foreign aid, a situation which it is predicted cannot last past the year 2000. And the expectation is that increasing numbers of West Indians will emigrate to Miami, New York and London. "With our tourism, abundance of minerals, oil, timber and other resources, we should be in the same development league as Malaysia, Singapore, Korea and Taiwan . . . ". We ought to be among the largest industrial nations in the Americas and could, in our own right, be an important contributor to the world's goods or to the world's raw materials.
>
> We can also become a great trading bloc, and could in two decades at most, enjoy the highest standard of living of any grouping in the world. And given peace and security no CARICOM national should have anything but the highest confidence about his region, his world and his destiny.

One can forgive a certain hyperbole, given the occasion for which the speech was made, but the speaker made a point of fundamental importance.

THE RESPECTIVE ROLES OF THE PUBLIC AND PRIVATE SECTORS

All member states of CARICOM now agree that the state (as a general rule, but subject to exceptions) should not be involved in direct production of goods and tradeable services and that there must be an enhanced role for the private sector in national development. Indeed, the practice of privatisation of public utilities and state corporations is gaining ground. The precise method of privatisation often raises complex issues, but there should always be opportunities for the employees of the enterprise to own shares in the privatised firm.

Experience (rather than economic theory or political ideology) has shown the lack of success of many state-owned and managed public utilities and state enterprises in developing countries. Privatisation does therefore make sense and as a result there are likely to be fewer state-owned utilities and enterprises in the future. There is also a place for management contracts combined with part state ownership.

However, the state will always have one obvious and indispensable role: sound national macroeconomic management and medium- and long-term development policies and programmes.

There should be closer cooperation between the state and the private sector in West Indian economic development and integration. They could jointly identify new industries and enterprises and modernise existing enterprises which seem to have good export prospects. Alternatively, the private sector could be left to perform the task by itself. The state will then have to facilitate the establishment of such enterprises, if found to be viable, for example, by fiscal incentives, export credit and protection.

THE PSYCHOLOGICAL AND CULTURAL ASPECTS OF CARICOM

Clearly integration groupings exist in order to assist in the national development of the member states. But, if integration is to be successful, there are some intangible factors which cannot be overlooked.

While integration cannot be the dominant force in promoting national development, it can make a very useful contribution. Non-economic factors help to accelerate the integration process as well as the process of national development, since without the will to integrate, there will be the same stagnation as is produced at the national level by the lack of political will, of private-sector energy, of proper attitudes by the workforce and of participation at the local community level. The relationship between non-economic and economic factors is reciprocal.

If, in spite of national differences, large numbers in each country feel a sense of kinship and affinity with the people of other member countries in the grouping, this would be good in itself.

Is CARICOM a means to National Development or an end in itself?

The answer is both. Strong economic cooperation and integration cannot be achieved unless the participants share a "sense of community" (to use the words of Roderick Rainford, a former secretary-general of CARICOM). To facilitate the functioning of any integration grouping, widespread commitment to the movement must be present in all member states.

The situation is very similar to the human resource development problem. Human resource development is an end in itself in that it develops and brings out the full potential of persons. This is of great value in itself, but it is also the most important means of bringing about economic development in the contemporary world.

If one views monetary integration (with or without a common currency) as a symbol of West Indian community, it is a good thing in itself. It can also be a means to achieve macroeconomic stabilisation and development at the individual country level, judging from the experience of the ECCB serving the seven OECS countries. Exchange rate changes are more likely to be infrequent since they have to be unanimously agreed and there are strict limits on government borrowing from the central bank.

Identity, Culture, Ideology and Sovereignty

The questions of identity, culture and sovereignty have to be given their due weight in discussing both national development and economic integration. These concepts are concerned with motivation, just as the output and quality of work by people in an organisation depend on motivation and not necessarily just the wages. The political directorate and top managers in both the private and public sectors and those trained in the principles of management and public administration are fully aware of these cultural and psychological motivations.

We in the West Indies are part of western civilisation, but in our view a very special and unique part. We came from many different parts of the world, most of us against our wish. Yet there has been an inevitable process of creolisation affecting all the people in our countries, starting with the first European settlers. There has over the centuries been a shaping of an underlying common West Indian culture in spite of national and ethnic differences.

> The Caribbean, mingling as it does the cultural legacies of Africa, Europe, Asia and indigenous America, is the epitome of New World Civilization.

This extract from a recent statement by Owen Arthur, prime minister of Barbados, to the Miami summit (December 1994) is full of insight and relevance.

Our common cultural identity is due to many factors: the English language, our common history, the sugar plantation, slavery and indentureship, the highly restrictive suffrage and representative system of direct Crown Colony government, common legal and administrative systems and patterns of social stratification. In two of the bigger countries, there are Indian as well as African cultural components.

The presence of varied elements in a country tends to increase creativity and versatility.

The contact of the last 150 years has had a great effect. Graduates of UWI from the different countries have developed relationships with West Indians from other countries. In the diaspora a similar situation exists through flourishing international sport; cricket is a powerful unifying force, although from time to time it gives rise to minor family quarrels among countries. The international lure of reggae, the steelband calypso and soca is important, and the development of a distinct West Indian literature should also be stressed. Important work in knitting the region together has been done by CANA, CBU programmes, such as CARIBSCOPE, and CAMWORK. The Caribbean electronic media have recently jointly rented space on a satellite to assist in disseminating programmes and news to each other and to the outside world.

In two of the larger countries, Guyana and Trinidad & Tobago there is a rough balance between two major ethnic groups which together form the vast bulk of the population. It is right and proper that they should try to hold on to the remaining cultural roots from the countries from which their ancestors came. However, the leaders (political, religious, intellectual, professional and cultural) of these two groups are sophisticated and far-sighted enough to understand the process of West Indian creolisation, which has had profound effects on both groups. It is impossible to reverse the deep historical currents making for creolisation except through the terrible blood-baths experienced in the Balkans and some African and Middle Eastern countries.

But we cannot afford to be unrealistic and take literally the saying that "all of we is one" within every country and between all the countries. In some democratic countries there is much "particularism" accompanied by genuine loyalty to the country. In the UK there is no conflict between being a Londoner or a Scotsman or a Welshman and being British. In the USA there is no conflict between being a Texan and being an American. Within a single nation-state today there are some cultural differences as between some parts of the country but no conflicting loyalties between one's particular region and the nation-state. Similarly, in many countries of the West Indies there is no conflict between being a Jamaican and a West Indian or in being a St Lucian and a West Indian or in being a Guyanese and a West Indian.

Many of us would like the West Indian aspect strengthened and to develop a greater sense of West Indian identity and feeling of kinship, but not at the expense of transferring completely our commitment to our own particular West Indian country. The West Indian cultural identity that runs through our countries should be strengthened both as an end in itself and as a means of deepening regional integration.

We all know that under the skin we all belong to the West Indian family, scattered over the Caribbean Sea and throughout the diaspora.[1]

Shridath Ramphal (the Chancellor of UWI) over the past 30 years has been calling for an ethos of West Indian regionalism, if the regional movement is to function properly. Ian Boxhill, sociology lecturer at UWI has recently published a pioneering book entitled *Ideology and Regional Integration in the Caribbean* in which he calls this an essential to promoting Caribbean economic integration, a view which is shared by this author.

Turning to the greatly misunderstood issue of sovereignty, it is important to distinguish between formal or purely juridical sovereignty and real or effective sovereignty. Individually the countries of the West Indies cannot exercise much by way of effective sovereignty in dealing with the outside world. To gain more it is necessary, particularly since independence, to voluntarily exercise some aspects of our sovereignty through CARICOM. We know from practical experience that our individual effective sovereignty is greatly enhanced when we act as a group in regional and international affairs. The obverse of this — also based on practical experience — is that when we act separately on matters of very important common interest, we not only weaken the effectiveness of our countries, but that of our sister countries in CARICOM as well. As John Compton, the former prime minister of St Lucia, has said on several occasions, "CARICOM is a shield for all of us and we should never fail to use it".

Economic Integration and Political Integration

Economic Integration

The economic integration, functional cooperation and the coordination of external trade policies and other aspects of foreign policy in CARICOM is one thing. But in order to deepen CARICOM a high degree of political cooperation is needed. Even under the loose and weak CARIFTA, the predecessor of CARICOM, there was much political cooperation. Under CARICOM, there has been a higher degree of political cooperation towards closer economic integration. It requires a close feeling of kinship to move from a Community or economic union of sovereign states to a single nation-state (whether federal or unitary).

In today's world a confederation is not political union but a league of sovereign states. Confederation is a strong form of integration, falling short of political union. Economic union requires great political cooperation but not political union. A confederation may be said to exist when among a group of countries there is economic union, monetary integration and a single foreign policy. If a confederation were to be relevant to the countries of the Eastern Caribbean there would need to be a wide range of common technical and administrative services as well.

The example of the EU is instructive. It is now moving towards an economic union including also a very high level of coordination of foreign and defence policies. But most of the member states and their people have not yet got attuned to the idea of political union – that is, a single European nation-state.

Political Integration

Political integration involves fundamental considerations. It requires the commitment of the people, the social partners and the political leaders of the various member countries to go beyond a single market (economic union) or a confederation.

The OECS, on an initiative of Sir James Mitchell, prime minister of St Vincent and the Grenadines, and John Compton, the former prime minister of St Lucia, has been attempting in recent years to form a political union. But only the four Windward Island governments (Dominica, Grenada, St Lucia and St Vincent and the Grenadines) have actively taken part in discussions. The three smaller Leeward Islands (Antigua and Barbuda, Montserrat and St Kitts and Nevis) have neither yet expressed interest in the proposal nor have they formally rejected it. It would be desirable and practicable for the OECS countries to form a political union, because, apart from the intrinsic advantages, this would be fully consistent with the deepening of CARICOM.

In 1991 Patrick Manning, the then prime minister of Trinidad and Tobago, proposed in the Manning Initiative, closer union among the three southernmost CARICOM countries of the Eastern Caribbean – Barbados, Guyana and Trinidad and Tobago – within, the framework of CARICOM. Erskine Sandiford, then prime minister of Barbados, is reported to have said at the inter-sessional heads of government meeting in St Vincent in 1993, in answer to a question raised at a press conference, that he was thinking in terms of a confederation of the three individual member states (in which each member remains a separate nation-state) and, with the consent of the other two heads, would be working on a draft of this concept. These initiatives should not be seen as attempts to weaken CARICOM; rather they are likely to strengthen it. The three countries will continue to participate fully in CARICOM and in fact it might greatly facilitate and expedite the operations of CARICOM if the OECS were a single political sub-grouping.

There is no attempt being made here to exclude The Bahamas, Belize and Jamaica from any kind of West Indian confederation or political union that may emerge in the Eastern Caribbean. The major parties in these three countries have made it clear that while they fully support the deepening of CARICOM, they are not interested in forming a political union. One must respect their views; indeed, there is no alternative.

Some would argue that the most rational political system in the Eastern Caribbean would be a federation of the ten members of CARICOM plus the British Virgin Islands and Anguilla.

There have been several initiatives towards political union in the Eastern Caribbean. One was the Grenada Declaration of 1971 which proposed that all ten Eastern Caribbean states of CARIFTA should form a political union. This process was terminated before it really got started. In 1972 the late Arthur Lewis (former vice-chancellor of UWI) led a group of eminent West Indians (including the late Hugh Wooding, formerly chancellor of UWI) who proposed the establishment of a federation of all the Eastern Caribbean members of CARIFTA together with the British Virgin Islands.

A similar proposal for the entire Eastern Caribbean membership of CARICOM, but excluding the British Virgin Islands and Anguilla, was made in 1974 by a Trinidad and Tobago task force on relations with the Caribbean, chaired by the economist Fitz Francis who was appointed by Eric Williams, then prime minister of Trinidad and Tobago. The Francis task force came out in favour of a political union of the ten member states of CARICOM in the Eastern Caribbean.

Another initiative was taken by the government of Eric Williams financing a study team, chaired by Alister McIntyre, to examine the feasibility of a political union of the seven Leeward and Windward Islands. (The two other members of the team, both from the UWI staff were Vaughn Lewis and Patrick Emmanuel.) The team reported favourably on the proposal in 1975 and, as envisaged in Eric Williams' proposal, then reported to a small constitutional commission, led by Telford Georges, the West Indian jurist. The commission recommended a loose form of political union, but nothing came of them.

A more acceptable and relevant proposal in 1996 might be a federal union of all members of the OECS (plus Anguilla and the British Virgin Islands), along with the individual countries of Barbados, Guyana and Trinidad and Tobago, forming a West Indian confederation of four. If this worked, then the confederation might be converted into a political union of all ten present member states of CARICOM in the Eastern and South-Eastern Caribbean. However, an alternative arrangement might be a political union of Barbados and the OECS countries, which would be a single unit in a three-country confederation of the "Little Eight", Guyana and Trinidad and Tobago.

We have refrained from putting forward lengthy arguments in favour of political union in some or all of the ten Eastern Caribbean member states of CARICOM. Such arguments include those for moving to a single market and an economic union, common services and functional cooperation and for strengthening the coordination of foreign policy (or indeed having a single foreign and external trade policy) – except that they apply with greater force to the case of a political union since many actions will take the form of both legislation and executive decision by the central authorities.

It is important to draw attention to the great practical problem of allocating to the central authorities under either a federation or confederation responsibility for the very expensive social and human resource development services (mainly education and health). It could be agreed by the participating States that this should not happen for a very long period of time – although the central authorities could have pools of experts of many types in these two vital areas.

Arthur Lewis in his *Agony of the Eight* (1965), suggested that under a division of powers and a West Indian or region-wide judiciary, a federal political union, can most effectively serve to prevent tyranny or arbitrary government at the local or island level and to protect civil and political human rights. This is the "good governance" case for political union. But there is another aspect of the "good governance" case. This form of government can provide many administrative and technical services more effectively than if all these societies were left to operate on an island basis. Pools of experts could serve all the countries in the union.

Havelock Brewster, co-author with Clive Thomas of the path-breaking study *The Dynamics of West Indian Integration*, Social and Economic Studies (1967), is now thinking more in terms of intangibles such as symbols of unity as an end and not only as a means of promoting economic development in the region.

Cheddi Jagan, president of Guyana, in a lecture in 1996 at the Institute of International Relations at the University of the West Indies (St Augustine) made a strong plea for a West Indian union which would not constitute a single nation-state, either federal or unitary. The principal result of his proposal would be symbolic and could help to create a greater sense of West Indian community. The union would involve a common West Indian citizenship; each person born in a CARICOM country would have dual nationality; that of the country of his birth and that of the West Indian union.

NOTE

1. For more on identity and culture, see the numerous writings of Rex Nettleford (See list of references). George Lamming has also made many highly perceptive contributions to this theme. See also the papers prepared by Lloyd Best and Stuart Hall referred to in the List of References. Kamau Brathwaite, C.L.R. James, Philip Sherlock, Eric Williams, Ian McDonald, Vidia Naipaul, Gordon Rohlehr and Kenneth Ramchand have also written extensively on this issue.

6

The Deepening of the Caribbean Community from Common to Single Market or Economic Union

This chapter deals with the specific ways in which the common market can be deepened into a single market or an economic union. Advance is necessary in the face of retrogression from the CARICOM treaty's obligations concerning intra-regional trade liberalisation and the CET, since there are still some obstacles to intra-regional trade and the CET has never been truly common to all. We need a great leap forward to move from our present situation to the creation of a single market or economic union.

At the same time we have to be much more active than in the past with regard to cooperation in production and marketing, in which the region's private sector has to play a major role.

MARKET INTEGRATION

One approach to economic integration involves removing all barriers to intra-group trade, the establishment of a CET and freedom of movement of the factors of production, that is, capital, entrepreneurship, management and workers with varying skills. In this scenario member states are called upon to consult on, and sometimes even coordinate, national economic policies and sector development programmes and work towards significant monetary cooperation.

The view that the provisions of the CARICOM treaty provide only for market integration and exclude cooperation in production is erroneous: the provisions of the Common Market Annex to the Treaty of Chaguaramas should be studied.

Protection, Reciprocity and the CET

Apart from full and effective intra-regional free trade subject to strictly enforced rules of origin, the CET is necessary as a means of protecting regional production. The issue is the degree of protection afforded by the height of the tariff. Most of the MDCs of CARICOM have already removed quantitative import restrictions, so that the CET is the only instrument of protection. The heads of government have agreed to phase the highest protective rate of duty in the CET down to 20 percent by 1998.

The elimination of quantitative restrictions and reduction in the CET have made life more difficult for the producers of agricultural and manufactured goods in CARICOM. But they will have to regard these measures as opportunities to develop exports to extra-regional markets. So quick and sweeping has been the reduction of protection by both quantitative restrictions and tariffs that we have made all reasonable concessions we can to the industrial countries. Must we now be left with absolutely no protective devices or revenue-raising import duties?

The degree of protection of the CARICOM market is central to the granting of reciprocity in trade agreements with developed countries, such as those in the EU, Canada and the USA. The world is not a level playing field and experience, economic analysis and considerations of international justice require a large measure of non-reciprocity in trade agreements between developed countries (such as those of the EU under the Lomé Convention, Canada under CARIBCAN and the USA under CBI)) on the one hand and associated developing countries on the other. With a somewhat higher tariff and the retention of quantitative restrictions on at least some products, CARICOM could approach trade negotiations secure in the knowledge that it possessed some bargaining power in order to protect the regional market. This would make reciprocity an easier issue for CARICOM to deal with.

The danger of over-protection by developing countries is real but some judgement must be applied to counteract rigid neo-liberal economic doctrines. 'An overdose of the best medicine can kill the patient' and moderation should be the motto of every economic adviser in West Indian countries because of our delicate economies and social fabric.

An argument in favour of a moderate tariff at the local or regional level for a grouping of small countries such as the member states of CACM and CARICOM is that a too high CET will perpetuate the existence of high-cost, inefficient "infant industries", so that investors in these inefficient, highly protected industries receive large "rents" from the domestic consumers of their product.

There are still some tariff and non-tariff barriers impinging on intra-regional trade. Obviously, such remaining illegitimate restrictions ought to be removed immediately.

Freedom of Movement of Factors of Production

A true single market or economic union makes provision for the free movement of capital, entrepreneurship, management, and either highly skilled and technical personnel or all labour so that resources can be pooled to facilitate specific acts of integration. The only grey area here (in the West Indies as well as in other groupings) is whether to make this happen first for skilled labour and entrepreneurial, managerial, professional and technical personnel and defer the free movement of unskilled and semi-skilled labour. However, there are no good grounds for restricting the free movement of unskilled or semi-skilled labour where there is a genuine need. For instance, over the last 15 years movement in and out of Antigua by Dominicans, unskilled and semi-skilled, has varied with employment opportunities in the former country: during periods of high labour demand in Antigua, Dominicans went there and got jobs and when economic activity in Antigua fell off, most of the Dominicans returned home. This suggests that labour movement between the two countries was largely self-regulating. It should be noted that the president of Guyana, Cheddi Jagan, has recently issued publicly an invitation to nationals of all CARICOM countries, whatever their levels of skill, to work in Guyana and he has also expressed an interest in having a large number of Haitians reside in Guyana.

Rights of Establishment and to Provide Services

In order to pool the resources of the common market, any enterprise producing goods should have the right to establish business in a member state other than its own. Similarly, any enterprise or person providing services in any member state should have the right to provide such services in any other member state. Integration entails that nationals of all other member states should be given the same treatment as nationals in any given member state. This means that there will be some discrimination in favour of nationals of member states vis-à-vis nationals of non-member states. As small and very small countries, we have to tread carefully in negotiating (preferably as a CARICOM group) investment and services, from high-technology goods and services to fast-food outlets and taxi ownership and operations.

Consultation on and Coordination of National Economic Policies

This is necessary for the successful and smooth operation of a common market, but is difficult to achieve in practice. Some national fiscal, monetary and economic policy measures such as increases in indirect taxes on particular products or changes in the exchange rate must remain confidential until they are publicly announced or until the actual announcement by the appropriate minister or the Prime Minister. Mutual trust and integrity are essential for the coordination of economic policies.

There should not be the same difficulty in co-ordinating national-sector development programmes and projects where these have implications for CARICOM, for example the joint development of natural resources, industrial, tourism and agricultural-sector programmes and individual national and regional projects.

A big problem is the fact that nationals of one CARICOM country need a passport to enter another CARICOM country, while a North American or European tourist needs only, say, a driver's licence. There is much complaint about the need to fill in exit and entry forms. The heads of government have agreed to stop these practices and many countries' passport desks now have CARICOM nationals in the same entry lines as their own nationals. It appears that travel for CARICOM nationals is beginning to improve, but perhaps too slowly.

Financial and Monetary Cooperation and Coordination

Where matters of policy are concerned, this concerns ministers of finance but the operational aspects could for the most part be the responsibility of the central banks, with the ministers of finance being informed before the technical operations are implemented. From the late 1970's there has been no intra-regional multilateral clearing or settlements except for a partial arrangement between Barbados and the OECS.

The CARICOM Multilateral Clearing Facility (CMCF) has been inactive and payments are made by the commercial banks in individual countries through the acquisition of foreign exchange. Nevertheless, the CMCF should at the appropriate stage be re-established. The commercial banks in the various countries of the region should, supported by the central banks, set the lead in ensuring convertibility among regional currencies by willingly accepting the currencies of other CARICOM countries. This acceptability would motivate firms and individuals to follow their lead.

It is clear that the recent linkage of the national stock exchanges of Barbados, Jamaica and Trinidad and Tobago has the capacity to develop gradually into a CARICOM stock exchange as part of the regional capital market proposed by Michael Manley during his brief third period as prime minister of Jamaica. The issue of either unification of, or fixed relationships between, national currencies within or outside a band raises very difficult analytical and operational problems. A phased scheme for moving towards closer harmonisation of exchange rates in stages (depending upon progress in economic stabilisation in all countries) was contained in the Report of the West Indian Commission and was adopted by the conference of the heads of government. With hindsight, it might well take time to become feasible. The paradox is that member states have to achieve economic stabilisation before there can be the degree of monetary integration that would improve exchange rate stability. We do need monetary integration, because it may be a condition precedent to achieving exchange rate stability and other forms of monetary stability. And once we have monetary integration our future prospects for exchange rate stability will be greatly enhanced.

It has been argued that all we need to do to facilitate intra-regional transactions and payments is to move to convertibility of our respective currencies one with another. This is worth doing. It is, however, in our view, too simplistic. We will be in a position to move to full convertibility and maintenance of regional exchange rates within certain bands when we have stabilised our economies in that:

- there has been no change in the exchange rate for a period of three years;
- foreign exchange reserves are sufficient to finance three months' imports; and
- the debt-service level is not above 15 percent of exports (and, it should be added, the fiscal deficit has been considerably reduced.

Convertibility requires the free movement of capital and uniform regimes of exchange controls on both current and capital account. This convertibility of currencies in the CARICOM countries actually means that we will have stabilised all the economies of the member states. We should, however, be wary of making capital movements totally free and becoming international financial centres, for in that way, as the recent experiences of Mexico and Argentina show, we can become vulnerable to capital flight.

Monetary integration with a single currency is possible, as the experience of the ECCB demonstrates. A multi-governmental Caribbean monetary authority can more easily impose severe limits on financing the fiscal deficits of governments and keep the common exchange rate fixed for very long periods. The assumption here is that the monetary authority would have to make decisions on a basis of unanimity and not all governments would wish to change the parity of the regional currency at the same time or to permit more lending to individual member countries more than they should. A common currency and a stable exchange rate would be easier to achieve from the beginning if the countries moved straight from a currency board system to a multi-governmental central bank, than trying to unify several different currencies with different exchange rates and different fiscal deficits.

Fiscal deficits, the money supply, interest rates, inflation and exchange rates are all closely interrelated. The exchange rate is the most unpredictable, being the most subject to uncertainty and psychological expectation. (If people believe that the exchange rate will fall, even though the economy is not in fundamental disequilibrium, that feeling in itself can bring down the exchange rate.) Experience of the last 20 years has shown that there is an absolute need for exchange-rate stability for economic stabilisation, growth and development, and deepening the integration process.

Company law has long been in need of harmonisation between CARICOM member states on the basis of more up-to-date approaches which some members have not yet adopted. There is also an urgent necessity for double taxation treaties between all the member states of the common market. Some progress is already being made on this.

COOPERATION IN PRODUCTION AND IN MARKETING: A NEW THRUST IN CARICOM

Another approach to economic integration is cooperation in production. This implies activating projects which combine or link resources (capital, natural resources, labour, management and entrepreneurship) among two or more member states, and is particularly important in developing countries.

Regional cooperation in infrastructure such as highways, railways, ports, shipping, air transport and electric power, is feasible provided that the specific geographical situations in a sub-regional grouping are appropriate. Because CARICOM is physically fragmented across the sea, opportunities for some of these forms of infrastructure cooperation, for example, railways, inter-country highways, and electricity will not arise. But much could be done in shipping, air transport, telecommunications and meteorological services.

But it cannot be sufficient to create a greater economic space through the use of these instruments. The creation of a single market and monetary and financial integration merely supplies opportunities by removing uncertainties. The private sector must be active. Producers and governments will often have to carry out certain specific acts of cooperation such as:

- the integration of production;
- joint ventures between parties in two or more member countries including foreign investors to produce for the regional and extra-regional markets;
- the establishment of regional trading companies by the private sector to undertake the difficult task of marketing in extra-CARICOM countries;
- cooperation in setting standards in production for both the intra- and extra-regional markets; and
- a regional industrial and production policy.

Integration of Production and Marketing

Integration of production occurs when the input of one member country is used to produce an output in another member country. A classic example of this was the aborted proposal in the 1970s to combine Jamaican alumina with power produced by Trinidad and Tobago natural gas in order to manufacture aluminium within the region, which itself could spin-off other downstream activities.

The idea of resource combination as a fundamental instrument of West Indian integration was first put forward in 1964 by Alister McIntyre. It was taken up by Norman Girvan and Owen Jefferson in an article entitled *Corporate versus Caribbean Integration*. It was applied to a wide range of economic activities, which *prima facie* appeared to be feasible for the West Indies, by Havelock Brewster and Clive Thomas (both of UWI at that time) in *The Dynamics of West Indian Integration* (1967).

The concept, partly because it seemed to involve some planning and state ownership and/or intervention, was denounced by the regional private sector and was therefore not reflected in the CARIFTA Agreement of 1968, even though in an Annex to the Agreement it was agreed that at a later stage the establishment of "integration industries" would be pursued. However, in 1973 the Treaty of Chaguaramas provided for both market integration and cooperation in production, including joint development of natural resources, the rationalisation of production in the region, cooperation in exporting and regional industrial programming. The treaty also contained many more facilitating provisions on production cooperation and integration, in manufacturing, joint development of natural resources, the rationalisation of agricultural development in the region and cooperation in tourism. The Treaty of Chaguaramas certainly goes well beyond the theory of neoclassical market integration. An interesting study by Girvan, Boxill, Samuel and Whitehead, on *The Integration of Production in CARICOM* was published in 1994.

Would-be exporters to extra-regional markets (particularly in the USA) have been aware of the great difficulty in meeting a single order from any big department store in the USA, Canada or the UK and have found that local producers cannot meet such orders individually, so that the only solution is to pool the production of the entire CARICOM grouping. Special trading companies could undertake this kind of operation for the whole region and also acquire expertise in marketing abroad. Standards will have to be harmonised and observed in practice.

A Regional Trade Information System: The need for CARTIS

One of the most important instruments for promoting exports to regional and to extra-regional markets would be the expansion of the CARICOM Trade Information Service (CARTIS), a CARICOM information system for marketing and industrial and trade information.

Since a country's (or region's) position in the world pyramid is defined by its capacity to compete in the world market, a sub-region like the Caribbean has to approach the challenges through the joint action of the constituent states together with similar joint action between the state and private enterprise.

The trading sector in the Caribbean has traditionally operated non-competitively in a regulated protectionist environment serving the needs of the local markets and trading internationally with established partners under preferential arrangements.

The high level of competition which has become the order of the day in world markets is possible through the utilisation of modern information technologies.

The exchange of information via electronic data transfer mechanisms has become a critical element in the transaction of global business. Companies and governments are ensuring that the necessary infrastructure is in place to facilitate this quick interchange of information and networking has become commonplace.

There is much to be gained by companies in a region using the services of a regional trade information system, which will serve to:

- foster intra-regional trade;
- stimulate joint action by small-scale companies in their efforts to produce the amounts and quality of products to respond to market demand;
- share in market research and market penetration studies;
- access and share external information in a timely and cost-effective manner;
- provide quality checks on information being accessed;
- provide inter-linkages with other regional and national trade information systems, so as to be able to assess the competition and to be able to identify joint-venture and other opportunities; and
- minimise the cost of on-line information access.

The establishment of such a system in the region started in 1989 with the establishment within CEDP of CARTIS, funded by UNDP and with contributions from other donor agencies and regional governments. The regional coordinating centre is now called the Caribbean Export Development Agency.

In order for the services to be sustained, the system is now being established as a commercial venture, where business agreements will be negotiated with the members of the information network, to share in the data collection activities and the marketing and sales of CARTIS products.

The system currently limits its activities to the production of databases as follows:

- companies: profiles of manufacturers, exporters and importers in the region;
- business opportunities;
- trade control measures; and
- trade statistics.

Access arrangements will be via:
- Caribbean On-line, a Barbados External Telecommunication (BET) information service;
- CARTIS trade fax service; and
- hard-copy document service.

It is necessary for the services to be utilised (and paid for) and for the private sector to be more involved in the development and management of the system as a commercial venture, so that the system can be further refined and sustained.

It is true that information services are available via other systems, for example Internet, which can provide global access to information and that the region through its telecommunication connections is geared more towards the industrialised countries than intra-regionally. However, the value of CARTIS is that information about the region is gathered and organized within the region. It is not yet accessible on the international electronic data exchange systems. In the near future the greater volume of the trade of the Caribbean will be intra-regional within the wider Caribbean (ACS).

CARTIS as part of CEDP has a pivotal role to play in the new export orientation of the Caribbean Community, provided it can continue to establish firm priorities in its work programmes.[1]

Joint Ventures and the CARICOM Enterprise Regime (CER)

The conference of heads of government recently decided to establish CER and Caribbean Industrial Programming Scheme (CIPS). There is now scope for the establishment of joint ventures among the private sectors of member states. Here the incentives under the CER would be useful.

However, CIPS does not seem of great priority in view of the financial inability of governments to invest in the financing of productive investments. Moreover, CIPS calls for the imposition of a high degree of protection for the industrial entities concerned. A better alternative to CIPS will be the formulation and implementation of a CARICOM industrial policy.

Regional Industrial Policy

Following the study of the integration of production in CARICOM (undertaken by Girvan *et al*), the major instruments of CARICOM's industrial policy, apart from appropriate macroeconomic policies and the improvement and maintenance of infrastructure facilities, should be:
- Tariff policies;
- Import policies;

- Export promotion policies;
- Credit policies, including export credit;
- Foreign exchange policies;
- Tax incentive policies;
- Technological policies;
- Manpower development policies;
- Policies affecting the supply of other inputs; and
- Policies and programmes for the development of extra-regional exports of goods and non-tourism services.

The Government of Jamaica has been working on an industrial policy. In March 1996 a paper was submitted to parliament for discussion which could serve as a very useful input into the formulation of a regional industrial and production policy.

These policy instruments should be harmonised, like the CET and the harmonisation of fiscal incentives to industry, now being revised. In addition, it is well-known that nearly all the instruments listed above were employed by Japan, South Korea, Taiwan and Singapore in their industrial development. Their use reflected the fact that industrial development can be achieved by the close working together of the state and the private sector, a rejection of the idea that development should be left solely to the market place and that there is or should be a level playing field. The state must intervene selectively, even if this creates what neo-classical and neo-liberal economists call distortions. Even a superficial acquaintance with the recent economic history of East Asian developing countries shows the importance of a symbiotic state-private sector approach.

It is also essential that the main thrust of fiscal incentives (or of the taxation system as a whole) should be to energise national and regional efforts towards exporting to extra-regional markets. This close working cooperation between private-sector entities and the state should be the single most important component of the new CARICOM. This indicates one of the ways in which CARICOM can help the development of the member states. To say this is not to say that there is no room for efficient regional import-substitution. What matters is that such substitution should be efficient; and the removal of quantitative restrictions and the big reduction in the Common External Tariff should ensure such efficiency.

Cooperation in Tourism

Auliana Poon has shown that tourism can be an axial product in CARICOM, capable of generating vertical, horizontal and diagonal linkages both nationally and regionally; these linkages can be with respect to both other services and industrial, agro-industrial and agricultural goods. In other words, with systematic efforts by both the government and the private sector, the tourism sector can be a basic "transformation" sector in our regional development.

Tourism in CARICOM, and even in the archipelagic Caribbean can benefit considerably from joint promotion and marketing abroad, as is now beginning to happen.

There are other areas of functional cooperation in tourism. One is the establishment and maintenance of a common position on the extent to which cruise ships can make a reasonable economic contribution to the economies of the member states of CARICOM. Another is training.

Cooperation in Agriculture

A far-reaching regional food plan, formulated by the CARICOM Secretariat, was adopted in 1975 by the conference of heads of government. It was sound both conceptually and operationally. Unfortunately, it was badly implemented by member states mainly because of lack of political will. One of the key elements, the Caribbean Food Corporation (CFC) was established but has never received or raised adequate financial support.

It is clear that cooperation in areas such as research and development, processing, marketing and transportation for both traditional and new agricultural crops makes good sense. This kind of cooperation would promote greater competitive efficiency.

There is considerable scope for cooperation in marketing and export promotion of new agricultural exports (tropical fruits, winter vegetables, cut flowers and tropical foliage, etc.) by the 'pooling of market intelligence, promotional efforts, and supply capabilities . . . Export marketing companies . . . exchange of technical information . . . and cooperation in R & D could also strengthen the technical base of production.'

The subject of local and regional import substitution in agriculture, is too complex to be dealt with here. We merely draw attention to the Caribbean Community Development Programme for Agriculture presented by the CARICOM Secretariat and adopted by the Standing Committee of Ministers of Agriculture. This document reviews production and marketing possibilities for specific types of agricultural activity within a regional framework and examines the institutional framework for promoting agriculture both nationally and regionally.

There is a useful role to be played by the CFC if it is better funded by the regional private sector and external financial agencies such as the European Development Fund (EDF). The public must recognise the importance of national and regional import substitution in agriculture, not only for economic reasons (strengthening the balance of payments and creating productive employment) but also for attaining greater food security.

Joint Development of Natural Resources

In view of the abortive attempt to develop jointly bauxite and energy resources to produce aluminium in the late 1970s, we must of necessity not think only of mega-projects with total or majority shareholdings by governments who today have no money for engaging in this kind of large-scale activity.

Instead, we should examine jointly-owned projects under private sector total or majority ownership and control. One possibility is a joint fishing and seafood venture using the waters of Guyana. A good example has been set by Ken Boyea, a dynamic entrepreneur from St Vincent and the Grenadines, who is importing unfinished rice from Guyana and processing it in St Vincent for final consumption. Arrangements have been made by a Trinidad and Tobago firm for processing Guyana's timber for sale in Guyana, CARICOM and other countries.

Finally, there are the possibilities of joint development of natural resources by enterprises owned by the regional and extra-regional private sector and targeted to the extra-regional market.

An Efficient and Reliable System of Sea and Air Transport

There are two reasons why the countries of CARICOM need an efficient and reliable air and sea transport system. One is that all the member countries are separated by the sea (which rules out the classical methods of inter-country roads and railways), which leaves air and sea transport as the options for cooperation in transportation. A reliable air transport system is needed to serve not only the needs of West Indian inter-country air travel for business and vacation purposes but also the important tourism industry.

The winding-up of WISCO (a shipping company owned by governments) has not profoundly affected the region since complaints by the regional private sector have been subdued. But we still need close cooperation in sea transport, as Jamaican Prime Minister, P.J.Patterson has recently pointed out, for training in all aspects of maritime transport, uniform up-to-date shipping legislation and joint policies on the cruise ship subsector of tourism.

Air transport is a more complex issue. The ideal situation would be a single air carrier serving both the internal and external needs of all the CARICOM countries. The most sensible form would be two CARICOM air carriers, with substantial ownership by both the regional private sector and by a reputable extra-regional carrier, with governments having a shareholding and appropriate representation on the board of directors of the companies. The governments and the regional private sectors would between them have at least 51 percent shareholdings and voting power. One would operate in the north-western part of CARICOM, linking, inter alia, Belize and the Bahamas with Jamaica directly. The other would serve the east and south-east Caribbean. The eastern and south-Eastern Caribbean carrier would have a department or subsidiary which would serve the intra-Caribbean route in the area.

Two airlines are now serving the intra-country needs of the eastern and south-eastern Caribbean: LIAT and Carib Express. It is to be hoped that cooperation between the two will have a positive effect on the efficiency and profitability of LIAT. Already there are signs that LIAT is operating more efficiently under a new board of directors and new management.

It is one of the weaknesses of both CARIFTA and CARICOM that over a period of more than 30 years, we have singularly failed to establish an efficient, rational and profitable regional air transport system. Recent developments mean that we can now wait and see what happens next. The suspension of the services of CARIB Express might provide yet another opportunity for rationalisation.

One company owned by a CARICOM member state in the south-eastern Caribbean and the majority of the people of that country perceive themselves as being treated less favourably than the spirit of integration would have required. One can only hope that in future there will be more regional cooperation regarding this airline, particularly as to the maintenance (and even expansion) of route rights which other CARICOM countries have extended to it. Although foreign investors now participate in the airline, it is still substantially owned and effectively controlled by the country concerned.

STRENGTHENING OF COMMON SERVICES AND FUNCTIONAL COOPERATION

The heads of government as already noted, have decided to establish a Caribbean Community Court of Appeal as a Court of final jurisdiction for the region and to have it replace the Judicial Committee of the Privy Council in London. Apart from being an expression of our true sovereignty, this action should also do much to create a West Indian jurisprudence. It is expected that the court will come into existence within a reasonably short period of time. The West Indian Commission strongly supported this decision by the conference of heads of government.

The heads of government also decided, on a proposal by Erskine Sandiford, then prime minister of Barbados, to establish a CARICOM Assembly drawn from the national parliaments of states. Perhaps social partners could have been included. The assembly would be deliberative rather than having the power to pass legislation and could create an important forum for the public discussion of important CARICOM (but not national) issues.

There is undoubtedly scope for a standing forum of social partners drawn from governments and opposition, employers, the trade unions, regional women and youth groups, the Church and other non-governmental organisations (NGOs), to meet once every two years to discuss matters of fundamental importance to the development of CARICOM and its member states. It will be recalled that A.N.R. Robinson, former prime minister of Trinidad and Tobago, called a successful meeting of these groups in Port-of-Spain in 1990. All the participants at that meeting were of the view that such a forum should continue to meet every two years.

The West Indian Commission also recommended the adoption by all governments of a CARICOM charter of civil society, setting out some of the fundamental principles required for the good governance of the countries of the region. The heads of government accepted this recommendation and a final draft is being prepared by the CARICOM Secretariat for submission to the conference of heads of government.

MAKING THE COORDINATION OF FOREIGN POLICIES MORE EFFECTIVE

Over the last few years it has emerged from heads of government conferences that greater efforts could be made to coordinate the foreign policies of member states. It was also agreed that a very important step forward would be for all the CARICOM governments to amalgamate, or share the costs of, some existing embassies and in appropriate cases establish joint embassies. For example, why should there be more than one CARICOM embassy in places such as Brussels, Geneva, Ottawa, Caracas, Mexico City, Lagos and New Delhi? Another but less good proposal is to group CARICOM embassies in some capitals into a single building sharing common services.

NOTE

1. Earl Baccus, director of the Caribbean Export Development Agency and Carol Collins, director of the CARICOM Secretariat, were helpful to the writer in this section. They should not, however, be held responsible for its contents.

7

The LDCs, The OECS and the Caribbean Development Bank

Like in all groupings, polarisation between MDCs and LDCs was initially seen as a great difficulty. The Caribbean Development Bank (CDB) was a major instrument for compensating the LDCs and reducing polarisation between LDCs and MDCs. (There were other measures in the Treaty of Chaguaramas designed to combat polarization which will be mentioned later in this chapter.). Although most of the resources available to the CDB (both ordinary capital, hard funds, and concessional capital, soft funds, came from outside CARICOM, the Bank was seen by the LDCs, when they signed both the CARIFTA Agreement and the CARICOM Treaty as an essential instrument of the broad process of West Indian integration. They would probably have acceded to neither CARIFTA nor to CARICOM without the creation and operation of this instrument to combat polarisation.

From the start of the negotiations on CARIFTA in 1967, the small and less developed countries (the Windward and Leeward Islands and Belize) pressed very hard for the establishment of the CDB as a source of soft loans for funding infrastructure projects badly needed in their countries. All the present members of CARICOM (including Belize, which joined CARIFTA in 1972 and CARICOM in 1974) are also borrowing members of the CDB.

The CDB was established by the Kingston Agreement of 1969 and initially all the member countries of CARIFTA joined as borrowing member countries. Two non-regional and non-borrowing countries, Canada and the UK, were founding members, to be followed by two non-borrowing regional members, Colombia and Venezuela, in 1973 and 1974 respectively. Later on, Mexico joined, also as a non-borrowing regional member.

Subsequently, other OECD countries joined: France, Germany and Italy. The USA, the Netherlands and Sweden have made substantial contributions to the special funds or soft resources of the CDB, but have not joined as full members. A very large amount of the soft money has gone to the LDCs which comprise some 11 percent of the total population of all the borrowing member countries. Moreover, for the first ten years of the CDB's operation, the more developed countries abstained from borrowing from the Special Development Fund (the major soft fund of the CDB) so that the LDCs had sole rights to borrow soft funds. As a result of the CDB's sound fiscal management, combined with bilateral support from both member and non-member donor countries, the infrastructure (seaports, airports, electricity, main roads, farm-access roads, water supply and distribution, telephones) of the LDCs has expanded and improved substantially since the CDB began operations.

The LDCs have borrowed global lines of credit from the CDB for passing on to their national development banks (or finance corporations) which have made sub-loans directly to small-scale and medium-scale private-sector enterprises. From its inception, the CDB also lent directly to the larger private-sector projects.

The Windward and Leeward Islands in 1981 participated in forming the OECS which looks after many of their special needs, in addition to CARICOM, for functional cooperation, economic integration and joint external policies and actions. The OECS has been very successful. But this success has not been matched by firm moves to political integration, a necessity for these very small countries in close proximity to each other which have very much in common.

One important initiative has been taken by the governments of the four Windward Islands. They have decided to form the Windward Islands Banana Development Company (WIBDECO), which is a company operating under the company law of each country. The shares in the company will be held on a 50:50 basis by the four governments and by persons and firms involved in the banana industry. It will resume the practice of bulk buying from overseas supplies of inputs, including fertilisers, so as to lower the costs to farmers. It will also be more directly involved in the marketing of the bananas overseas, principally in the UK market.

The Treaty of Chaguaramas made special provisions for the LDCs. Some of these are as follows.

- Protection for new industries in the LDCs against competition from existing industries in the MDCs (except for Barbados), which were to have no right to keep out the products of such industries. Twenty-six industries in the LDCs have obtained this benefit.
- Longer periods of fiscal incentives for the LDCs than for the MDCs.

- The phasing-in periods for the CET were longer for the LDCs from a position of 55 percent commonality with the MDCs in 1973.
- The Agricultural Marketing Protocol, the Oils and Fats Agreement and the Guaranteed Markets Scheme, by which more local and regional foodstuffs could be supplied to all CARICOM countries by the LDCs.
- Technical cooperation between the MDCs and the LDCs.
- The establishment of a Caribbean Investment Corporation (CIC) with the participation of only the CARICOM countries, financed heavily by the MDCs, for funding equity for new industrial and tourism projects in the LDCs. The CIC was very active in discharging its mandate, but it had to be wound up in 1984 because the volume of loan financing was too small in comparison with the amount of equity financing provided for projects by it. The ratio of equity to loan financing provided by the CIC in the 1970s and early 1980s was 80:20 when it should have been 30:70.

According to the treaty all members of CARICOM were to intensify their efforts to promote the special interests of the LDCs in external trade negotiations and in obtaining development finance on appropriate soft terms. This has been, and is still being, done in the case of access of their bananas to the EU. Another important step was that the LDCs should (at least over the next few years) not be obligated to extend tariff reciprocity to Colombia under the recently signed trade agreement between Colombia and CARICOM.

All these special measures in favour of the LDCs (which included Belize) were readily agreed to by the MDCs, in addition to the foregoing of soft loans from CDB in favour of the LDCs for more than a decade.

Very obviously the LDCs also gain from the operation of CARICOM-wide common services and functional cooperation and foreign policy (including external trade policy) coordination, and it cannot be denied that the LDCs are better off within CARICOM than outside it. This meets the acid test, as Alister McIntyre pointed out some 30 years ago, of whether any participant country in an integration grouping should judge the net benefits (many of them intangible) of participation in the grouping.

We end by calling for a change of designation. Instead of talking about less developed and more developed countries, we suggest that the terminology be more neutral: say, Group A and Group B countries.

NOTES

1. For more on this issue see Rosina Wiltshire's study on Movement of Labour between CARICOM countries. See List of References.
2. On this section, we consulted Earle Baccus, director of the CARICOM Export Development Project and Carol Collins, director of systems information of the CARICOM Secretariat, who at one time headed CARTIS. However, we take full responsibility for what follows.
3. This list is taken from Norman Girvan, et al., on *The Integration of Production in CARICOM*.
4. Belize, although important to CARICOM, is classified as a less developed member country, both by CARICOM and by the CDB but is for obvious geographical reasons not a member of the OECS.

8

The Widening of the Caribbean Community

> We must strengthen the inner circles in order to survive; move to wider circles of regional cooperation if we are to hold our own; and press on to ever-widening circles of international cooperation if we are to concern ourselves not merely with survival and keeping up with the rest but with the advancement and relentless onward march of the people whom we claim to represent and who expect us through this institution to show them clearly the way ahead.
>
> (Extract from Chairman's Statement at 1975 Annual Meeting of the Board of Governors of the Caribbean Development Bank, (the late) Errol Barrow, then prime minister of Barbados)

THE WIDENING OF CARICOM IS NOT A NEW IDEA

The concept of widening CARICOM, or, more precisely, establishing a Caribbean Economic Community to include the entire Caribbean archipelago (plus Belize, Suriname and Guyana), is not a new one. Some 300 years ago a French priest, Father Labat, wrote about the essential unity of the islands of the "Antilles" in spite of the different languages spoken.

In January 1962, the late Eric Williams, after the collapse of the West Indian Federation, called for the creation of an Economic Community of the states and territories of the Caribbean archipelago together with Suriname, Guyana and Belize (the last two of which were not in the Federation). In 1975 he put a proposal to an annual ministerial meeting of the UN ECLAC, to establish a permanent ministerial committee to promote closer cooperation and integration among the countries of the Caribbean archipelago, with Belize, Guyana and Suriname. He himself was aware of the difficulties of the enterprise, differences in: languages, shades of culture, administrative and legal systems, country economic status, size and constitution (many of the territories being not yet independent).

Franklin Knight, a West Indian who is now Professor of History at Johns Hopkins University, has written a book on the history of the countries of the Caribbean archipelago entitled *The Growth of A Fragmented Nationalism*. This is an accurate way of describing the history of the Caribbean area that would probably have appealed to Eric Williams who covered broadly the same ground as Knight in his own history of the Caribbean archipelago entitled *From Columbus to Castro*.

Alister McIntyre's study, *Prospects of Trade and Development Policy for the Caribbean (Archipelago)* written for the IDB in 1964 is relevant as well.

It is worth noting that the written CARIFTA Agreement (1968) had the following quotation on its flyleaf: 'Towards the creation of a viable economic community of Caribbean territories'.

SOME BASIC DIFFICULTIES IN WIDENING CARICOM

An important consideration in the Caribbean archipelago is the fact that all the CARICOM countries have small populations compared with the countries of the Greater Antilles, that is, Haiti and the Dominican Republic with just under 7 million people each and Cuba with 11 million. Even Jamaica (2.4 million) would be thought small (with only 10 percent of the total population) in an economic community restricted to the independent countries of the Greater Antilles, whose total population - excluding Jamaica - is 29 million). The entire population of the independent countries of the Caribbean archipelago is 31 million.

Belize has an area of 23,000 square kilometres and Guyana's is 215,000 square kilometres with populations of 150,000 and 800,000 respectively. The whole of CARICOM as it is now constituted has a combined population of some 5.7 million people. If we include all the islands and all the mainland countries with a littoral on the Caribbean Sea, CARICOM with a population of only 6 million would have just under 3 percent of the total pan-Caribbean population of just over 200 million.

There are also wide differences of a constitutional and administrative character between countries and territories of the archipelago.

For these reasons, *inter alia*, CARICOM must be deepened and become more cohesive and unified in its external trade, economic and diplomatic relations, in order to smoothly achieve an economic community (as distinct from any looser forms of economic and trade cooperation) of the entire archipelago.

THE LEGACY OF OUR HISTORY: THREE CARIBBEANS

CARICOM peoples (or West Indians) are well aware that the Caribbean area is not confined to the former British colonies in the Caribbean. It is appreciated that the term "Caribbean" includes all the islands in the Caribbean archipelago (as well as Belize on the Central American mainland and Guyana and Suriname on the South American mainland).

Shridath Ramphal some 20 years ago from a West Indian point of view said that he saw the Caribbean in terms of "ever-widening circles of kinship":
- CARICOM;
- CARICOM plus the entire Caribbean archipelago; plus
- the mainland countries with a Caribbean littoral, namely Venezuela, Colombia, Central America and Mexico.

Let us call these circles of kinship:
- CARICOM or the West Indies;
- the Caribbean area (or archipelago); and
- the pan-Caribbean.

The USA calls the Caribbean area plus the Central American countries the Caribbean basin.

About 20 years ago, the late Errol Barrow, then prime minister of Barbados, stated to the 1975 meeting of the board of governors of the CDB, 'We must strengthen the inner circles', referring to the West Indian/CARICOM circle. But he went on to call for closer relationships between the "inner circle" and the two other circles of the Caribbean and the wider world.

This is an essentially West Indian perspective and does not imply any hostility or coldness to the wider Caribbean. It may spring from the very small populations and land space (with the exception of Belize and Guyana) of the present CARICOM. In this section we shall use the terms CARICOM, the Caribbean archipelago and the pan-Caribbean. In nearly all the mainland countries with a Caribbean littoral there are pockets of people of West Indian descent living on the coast and these could be a source of linkage for West Indian cooperation with the mainland.

In the pan-Caribbean, what binds us together is our common heritage of European political and economic colonialism and, above all, the Caribbean Sea. West Indians have a common culture, history, language and historical economic organisation (the sugar plantation, slavery and indentureship).

In the proposed pan-Caribbean ACS (including both the archipelago and the littoral) the whole of CARICOM would represent only an extremely small proportion of the total population at 3 percent.

The CARICOM countries should not be forgiven for the present lack of closer cultural and human ties with the rest of the Caribbean area and the mainland countries. Like our former English colonial masters, even after (in some cases) 30 years of political independence, the educated West Indian (with very few exceptions) still remains wholly ignorant of the Spanish, French and Portuguese languages and the history and culture of the wider Caribbean and Latin America. This is unfortunate and should be remedied without further delay by the West Indian authorities and by the people themselves.

THE MEANING OF WIDENING IN THE CARICOM CONTEXT

In view of the differences among the countries of the pan-Caribbean region, it is clear that widening CARICOM in this context cannot mean simply increasing the number of full member states. The disparities in size, range of natural resources and population and the differences in the legal, administrative and constitutional framework and in languages must all be taken into account.

Accordingly, the term widening has to have a different connotation from the way in which it has been used in integration movements such as CARICOM.

One cannot see in the foreseeable future a very deep formal integration between CARICOM and the mainland countries, going far beyond full or partial free trade and other forms of economic and technical cooperation. But if the FTAA is to be approached on a sub-regional basis, we can visualise a series of full or partial free trade areas between all the sub-regional groupings in the hemisphere, that is, CARICOM, NAFTA, the CACM, the Andean Group and Mercosur. In this way CARICOM would have trade liberalisation links with all of Latin America (including the ACS) and with North America. Thus, once the FTAA is established it will result in free trade between all ACS members. This is really to advocate the widening of CARICOM to include most of the Caribbean archipelago.

When referring to the non-CARICOM islands of the Greater Antilles, however, there is a case for using traditional terminology of "widening". One of the northern islands has 11 million people and the other two have just under 7 million each compared with CARICOM with a total population of 6 million. All these countries after a period of a *sui generis* economic and technical cooperation agreement (including full or partial free trade) with CARICOM, could move to full membership of CARICOM.

There is a very strong case for specific, practical forms of cooperation among the countries of the pan-Caribbean, in trade, finance, science and technology, culture, education and training. The ACS has great potential for considerable functional cooperation among all its member states.

With one or two exceptions, the relationship between the countries and sub-regional groupings of the ACS in the beginning must be *sui generis*.

THE RELATIONSHIPS BETWEEN DEEPENING AND WIDENING

These relationships can be stated in summary form as follows.
1. Intra-CARICOM deepening should proceed faster, so as to achieve a single market and economic union within a short space of time – by the year 2000.
2. The motto for CARICOM countries should be "Deepen quickly while beginning to widen". For the deepening of CARICOM, see the special meanings in Chapter 6. Widening must mean informal economic cooperation, including

trade and economic cooperation based on partial or total free trade agreements between CARICOM and other sub-groupings and countries within the ACS and the rest of South America, preferably with other sub-regional groupings rather than individual countries.
3. The secretariats of CARICOM, OECS, ACS, SELA, ECLAC, the CACM, the Andean Group and the Group of Three (Mexico, Colombia and Venezuela) should meet regularly to review trends and exchange views on trade and development.
4. CARICOM and its associate institutions (such as UWI, CDB and CARDI) should meet regularly with their counterpart institutions in the other ACS countries to help each other with their problems.
5. Countries should exchange views and experiences on all forms of financial flows: soft and hard loans from international and sub-regional institutions and bilateral donors, foreign direct and portfolio investments and new financial facilities and mechanisms.
6. The partners in joint ventures and the integration of production in which nationals of a CARICOM country are involved, should include nationals of both CARICOM and other ACS countries.
7. CARICOM countries should treat direct and portfolio foreign investments from other pan-Caribbean countries in the same way that they treat intra-CARICOM private flows, that is, as if they were national investors.
8. CARICOM and the other ACS Caribbean countries should collaborate (mainly through sub-regional and regional institutions) in the transfer and adaptation of technology so as to assist each other in their export drives to each other and to other countries of the world.

PRINCIPLES WHICH SHOULD GOVERN ECONOMIC RELATIONSHIPS BETWEEN CARICOM AND THE OTHER COUNTRIES OF THE ACS

1. The ACS is now in existence, based on a broad framework convention, covering areas and forms of cooperation among them.
2. Cooperation should cover cultural exchange, education and training, technology and science, the Exclusive Economic Zones, environmental and anti-pollution action and anti-drug activities and trade, financial and economic matters.
3. To the maximum possible extent much of the activities of the ACS should be in the form of inter- and sub-regional groupings. The Miami summit gave the hemispheric sub-regional groupings an important role in linking up with each other so as to facilitate the FTAA.
4. An individual CARICOM state should not seek individual membership of other regional sub-groupings (CACM, the Andean Group and Mercosur), since this would weaken CARICOM and possibly lead to its collapse.

5. CARICOM, with the smallest countries of the pan-Caribbean, needs to exercise intra-CARICOM actions and common policies within the framework of the ACS.
6. Member states should see the Caribbean Sea as a joint legacy of history and geography and jointly exploit, police and exercise surveillance over it concerning environmental, pollution and drug-related matters.
7. The member states of the ACS should strongly prohibit their marine police, coastguards, national guards, navies and fishermen from violating each other's territorial seas and from using force or violence against fishermen who are fishing inside their own territorial waters.
8. The member states of ACS should collaborate in science and technology and, where feasible, establish joint common services for this purpose.
9. For the medium and longer term some joint exploration, exploitation and surveillance of the Exclusive Economic Zones of member countries should be considered.
10. Movement towards widening should be carefully phased so as to smoothly mesh with the deepening of CARICOM.
11. Cooperation in external trade and other economic issues where there are common interests should be pursued by all ACS members.
12. CARICOM trade and economic agreements with individual Latin American countries (or preferably with sub-groupings of them) must give special regard to the interests of CARICOM's LDCs, particularly the OECS. This was achieved in the CARICOM/Colombia free trade agreement, in which the OECS countries will not be obliged to give tariff reciprocity to Colombia for the entire duration of the agreement (five years). In the CARICOM/Venezuela free trade agreement non-reciprocity applies to all CARICOM countries.

These guidelines and principles are reflected in the text of the ACS Convention recently signed in Cartagena.

SOME RECENT STEPS IN ECONOMIC COOPERATION BETWEEN CARICOM AND OTHER PAN-CARIBBEAN COUNTRIES

Many practical steps have been taken on all sides to bring the countries of the pan-Caribbean into closer trade and other economic relationships with each other.

The CARICOM member countries greatly appreciate that the three big mainland countries have themselves initiated acts of trade, financial and technical cooperation with the CARICOM countries as well as with non-CARICOM countries in the archipelago. These acts of cooperation include the following.

1. The San José Accord under which Mexico and Venezuela supply petroleum to some MDCs and LDCs of CARICOM on concessional terms.

2. The establishment by CARICOM of joint commissions with Mexico, Venezuela, the Dominican Republic and Cuba (in the last two the initiative was taken by CARICOM. It is interesting to record the fact that in 1973 Mexico offered to form a joint commission with Guyana. Guyana responded by proposing that a Mexico/CARICOM Commission be established and this was accepted. This concrete act of regionalism speaks well for Guyana's commitment to West Indian integration).
3. In the early 1970s Colombia and Venezuela became non-borrowing members of the CDB, contributing generously to both its ordinary capital resources and to the Special Development Fund. Venezuela established a trust fund of the then equivalent of US$50 million in the CDB. Since there are also some non-regional countries in the CDB (Canada, UK, France, Germany and Italy), this is an excellent example of cooperation between North and South and between South and South.
4. The three presidents of the Group of Three and the vice president of Suriname met CARICOM heads of state and government in November 1993 in Port-of-Spain, where they expressed agreement to the proposal for an ACS.
5. In 1975 the CARICOM countries, on the initiative of Eric Williams, pushed successfully for the establishment of a Caribbean Development and Cooperation Committee of ECLAC to focus on promoting economic and other forms of cooperation between the countries of the Caribbean archipelago.
6. The Trinidad and Tobago Government has reportedly recently decided to join the Andean Development Corporation, a development bank connected with the Andean Group, but with membership open to non-members of that Group. Some of the other members of CARICOM may do the same.

PAN-CARIBBEAN COOPERATION UNDER THE NEW
CONVENTION OF THE ACS

In the light of: the decision to deepen CARICOM and to promote pragmatic economic cooperation within the entire pan-Caribbean area; the small size of all the CARICOM member countries; the expressions and actions of the Group of Three; and not least the signing of the convention of the ACS, we tentatively suggest the following principles for guiding the operation of the proposed pan-Caribbean association.

Steps towards closer relations between CARICOM and the other countries of the ACS (both island and mainland), can be envisaged along the following lines.

1. CARICOM is quickly deepened so that by the year 2000 it can be transformed into a single market or an economic union. Simultaneously the widening process should be initiated. CARICOM should be the BENELUX of the ACS.

2. CARICOM group negotiation of partial or total free-trade agreements with the Group of Three, the Andean Group (which includes Venezuela, Colombia and Mexico), CACM and Mercosur, should start. In relation to the Andean Group, we should bear in mind that the vast bulk of production and trade comes from Venezuela and Colombia, with both of whom CARICOM as a group already has formal free trade agreements. In relation to Mercosur, we should remember that Brazil and Argentina are among the three biggest markets in Latin America.

3. After some deepening of all of the sub-regional groups, CARICOM the Andean Group, CACM and Mercosur, they should establish formal trade and economic links among themselves and with NAFTA and on that basis would eventually become part of the FTAA. The issue of reciprocity arises in this context. It is understood that under the Colombia/CARICOM free trade agreement, the OECS will not be required to offer tariff reciprocity. In all the negotiations with other countries and groupings in the hemisphere and in the EU, CARICOM must always seek to safeguard the interests of the OECS countries and, where necessary, Belize. The non-LDCs of CARICOM should also consider not granting full reciprocity to the above-mentioned sub-groups.

4. Collaboration in science and technology and in research and development throughout the pan-Caribbean.

5. Cooperation in education, training and health.

6. Cooperation in culture and language teaching.

7. Close collaboration among all the pan-Caribbean countries should include environmental protection, such as dealing with oil spills and nuclear waste affecting the Caribbean Sea – and therefore all pan-Caribbean countries.

8. Any act through which the territorial sea of any ACS state is violated by the armed forces and protective services of another ACS state should be scrupulously avoided, particularly when the use of firearms is involved.

9. CARICOM should develop, together with the independent countries of the Greater Antilles, proposals for some kind of trade and economic cooperation agreement (whether as part of the ACP countries or *sui generis*) with the EU to come into effect in 2001. (Perhaps an arrangement with the EU could be negotiated to encourage direct and portfolio foreign investment from Europe to the countries of the Caribbean archipelago.)

10. CARICOM should accelerate the formation of trade and economic links with the independent countries of the Greater Antilles with a view, if they so wish, to creating either a trade and economic agreement or associate and subsequently full membership of CARICOM.

11. Promoting mutual joint-venture capital flows between the CARICOM countries as well as between the countries of the pan-Caribbean.
12. Seeking to promote the integration of production with all the countries of the ACS, provided that proposed actions are always explored with the other CARICOM countries so that the integration of production amongst the CARICOM countries themselves is not pre-empted. But non-CARICOM pan-Caribbean investment in such projects should be encouraged.
13. There should be scope for CARICOM processing of raw materials and other intermediate goods from other pan-Caribbean countries for export to the EU, provided of course that enough value is added in the CARICOM countries.
14. CARICOM should try to consult other member countries of the ACS on matters of common interest before important hemispheric and world meetings are held.

It should be noted that at the first summit of the ACS held in 1995 the heads of state and government decided to embark upon programmes of cooperation in trade, transport and tourism.

CARICOM AND THE NON-INDEPENDENT CARIBBEAN TERRITORIES

We have not dealt with the future of the non-independent units of the Caribbean archipelago: Puerto Rico, the US Virgin Islands, the British Virgin Islands, Anguilla, Cayman Islands, Turks and Caicos Islands, the French Departments of Martinique, Guadeloupe and Cayenne, and the Netherlands Antilles. (Montserrat, although not yet independent of the UK, was a member of the West Indian Federation and CARIFTA, as it now is of CARICOM). The British Virgin Islands are associate members of CARICOM and of the OECS, and Anguilla is a member of the ECC. It would be in the interests of all concerned if Anguilla and the British Virgin Islands became full members of the OECS and associate members of CARICOM since we should seek to expand trade and other economic, technical and cultural cooperation with all the non-independent countries of the Caribbean archipelago. CARICOM should have informal trade and functional cooperation relations with them, and wherever feasible, involve them in CARICOM common services and in West Indian cultural expressions. Anguilla and the British Virgin Islands could become full members of the OECS and Anguilla could join the British Virgin Islands in some kind of relationship with the Caribbean Community. Should the Netherlands Antilles become independent, it could become an associate member and later full member of both the OECS and CARICOM. Some of these countries already enjoy observer status in institutions of CARICOM.

THE RELATIONSHIP BETWEEN CARICOM AND OTHER SOUTH AMERICAN COUNTRIES

What about those South American countries not included in the pan-Caribbean or the ACS?

There are a number of sub-regional integration groupings already in existence or being revitalised.

Examples are the Group of Three (Venezuela, Colombia and Mexico); the Andean Group (Venezuela, Colombia, Peru, Ecuador and Bolivia); and Mercosur (Argentina, Brazil, Uruguay and Paraguay). There is to be a CET in Mercosur and a partial free-trade agreement with it could in due course be negotiated by CARICOM. Much of this is in accordance with the role of sub-regional groupings as building blocks in the long-term good of the FTAA.

The first priority should be to deepen CARICOM, while exploring CARICOM links with other Latin American and Central American groups. We should not take actions that can fragment CARICOM, for example, by each or some CARICOM member state or states entering into partial or full trade and economic cooperation agreements with third countries or groupings of such countries whether located within or outside the hemisphere.

CONCLUDING REMARKS ON FREE TRADE AMONG ALL SUB-REGIONAL GROUPINGS IN THE WESTERN HEMISPHERE

The ACS was launched in 1995 shortly after the declaration of principles and plan of action of the Miami summit attended by all the chief executives in all the countries of the western hemisphere, except one. This declaration and plan calls for a deepening of the sub-regional groupings in the hemisphere (such as CARICOM) and the forging of closer trade and economic links among them (no doubt including NAFTA by inference), so that they can ultimately converge and the create FTAA.

Since nearly all the member states of ACS are parts of sub-regional groupings, the trade liberalisation aspect of the ACS will be difficult to implement. This is because, except for the three independent countries of the Greater Antilles, ACS member states will participate in the FTAA through links among these sub-regional groups. There will therefore be (by an indirect process) free trade among all the ACS countries (except for the three countries of the Greater Antilles just referred to). It is therefore desirable that CARICOM negotiates trade liberalisation and fuller integration with these three countries.

A strong impetus has been given to the deepening of CARICOM, since in order to forge mutually beneficial linkages with other sub-regional groups in the hemisphere, CARICOM must become more cohesive, both internally and externally.

The importance of deepening CARICOM and creating an economic union out of it is therefore extremely important as a means of preserving West Indian interests and the West Indian identity in the wider Caribbean hemisphere and the wider world. This having been said, the ACS has a very valuable role to play in trade and economic cooperation in the entire pan-Caribbean. The heads of state and government of the ACS have decided on cooperation in trade, transport and tourism as the priority areas for cooperation.

9

Towards a Coordinated External Trade Policy for the Caribbean Community

The Crucial Importance of External Trade Policy to CARICOM States

The Common Market section of the Treaty of Chaguaramas calls upon the member states to move towards the more specific task of "the progressive coordination of external trade policies". This aspect is a crucial, if not dominant, factor in CARICOM (and similar groupings). It is alien to the spirit and practice of regional or sub-regional groupings especially of a single market or economic union type if this coordination is not undertaken. One of the strengths of the EU is that on most occasions since the European common market was founded in January 1958, there has been constant coordination of external trade policy. The surest way to destroy CARICOM would be for individual countries to do their own thing in matters of external trade policy. We must never allow ourselves to be divided by the manipulation of powerful extra-regional groupings, countries or groups of countries. It is a matter of commonsense that the CARICOM countries should strive to retain an association with the EU, the USA (under CBI) and Canada (under CARIBCAN). It is also obvious that we should seek both to widen CARICOM and to develop trading links with the Latin American countries and non-English speaking Caribbean countries.

In 1969 Eric Williams, the then prime minister of Trinidad and Tobago, proposed a high-level ministerial mission to the European Commission and to all the member states of what used to be called the European Community in order to put the case for meeting the special interests of all the CARIFTA countries when the UK joined the Community. Eric Williams suggested that Robert Lightbourne, (the then minister of trade and industry in Jamaica) should lead the mission. All the CARIFTA member countries agreed and a single, coordinated CARIFTA mission was satisfactorily undertaken. Since then, it has been accepted that in matters relating to the formulation and implementation of external trade policy, CARICOM should act as one.

If any CARICOM countries negotiate individually, it is likely that the degree of reciprocity in respect of tariffs, government procurement and rights of establishment may vary in outcome. This would spell the end of coordinated CARICOM external trade, a unified CET and uniformity in rights of establishment and services in CARICOM. The policy of divide and rule of external, more powerful entities would triumph. Thus single-country or two-country approaches to NAFTA or FTAA will have serious adverse effects on CARICOM as a sub-regional grouping.

Individual CARICOM country negotiations would also weaken the bargaining power of other CARICOM countries, particularly the LDCs. Moreover, it could lead to the fragmentation of the CET and several other instruments of common policies towards the rest of the world. We should learn to take the long-term instead of the short-term view of our national and regional interests. (Just before sending this work to the publishers, I read the address delivered in late April 1996 by Owen Arthur, prime minister of Barbados, at the Distinguished Lecturer Series sponsored by the Institute of International Relations of UWI, St Augustine. It is an incisive and brilliantly expressed analysis of the rapidly changing external trade and economic environment of the CARICOM countries and the need for careful analysis of what should be done and for preparing for the undoubtedly complex set of negotiations ahead. The stress throughout is the need for group action by the CARICOM countries. (See List of References).

As individually small and weak countries, we should seek to maintain and enhance the diversity of our external trade and economic relationships. We should regard our present external links as windows of opportunity, to be used to good effect.

AN INVALID ARGUMENT ABOUT THE DISTRIBUTION OF BENEFITS OF TRADE LIBERALISATION AND INTEGRATION AMONG UNEQUAL PARTNERS

An argument has recently been advanced that in reciprocal free trade between a very big and a very small country, virtually all the gains accrue to the very small country and most of the losses to the very big country. The question is: why does the bigger and more developed country wish to have trade liberalisation agreements or deeper integration with a much smaller and less developed country. The answer may be that the bigger country is interested not only in trade but in other aspects of an economic cooperation agreement, which might include matters such as VIP treatment by the small country for investment services, government procurement and rights of establishment for the nationals of the bigger country.

The argument ignores the burden of the reallocation of factors of production and economic activities on the smaller country in this situation. The smaller countries, even if they gain in the long term, will face very severe costs of adjusting to the new situation.

This must be considered when CARICOM is negotiating with the EU, NAFTA and the bigger Latin American countries.

The argument leads to drastically different conclusions from those of modern development and international trade theory about the gains resulting from reciprocal free trade or deeper economic interaction between unequal partners. It runs counter to the polarisation argument of development economists such as Myrdal and Hirschman. It is well known that reciprocal trade liberalisation, deep economic integration and political union lead to more losses for the smaller and less developed countries than for the bigger and more developed ones, unless special measures for the smaller and less developed countries are adopted.

This argument would be more acceptable if the small and big countries were at similar levels of economic and human resources development, measured not only by high income per head and the use of advanced technologies but also by a diversified, resilient and flexible structure of production and exports, so that the gains might be more evenly shared. Unfortunately, the small countries of CARICOM, the rest of the Caribbean archipelago and Central America do not exhibit these characteristics.

All reciprocal free-trade areas, deeper forms of integration and unitary or federal nation-states characterised by wide internal disparities in levels of development (even where there is free movement of labour and capital) implement anti-polarisation measures such as direct, indirect and non-reciprocal fiscal transfers for the less developed parties. This is true in varying degrees of the GSP, CBI, CARIBCAN, the EU, the Andean Group, CACM and Mercosur. It is also true of unitary and federal nation-states such as the USA, Canada, Brazil, India, Germany, Japan, France and the UK.

HAS CARICOM BECOME SUPERFLUOUS WITH THE ESTABLISHMENT OF THE ACS?

> The scale of this operation is so considerably larger than CARICOM that many people have already begun to wonder whether this does not mean, step-by-step with the realisation of the new Association, a corresponding erosion of the existing CARICOM . . . Inevitably, CARICOM will be affected by these developments (the formation of the ACS), but it has the strength and the resilience to adapt, to adjust and to grow, in response to the robust development of its brainchild.
>
> (Extract from statement made on April 10, 1995 by Patrick Manning, former prime minister of Trinidad and Tobago, in Kingston, Jamaica)

Reading the relevant sections of the Report of the West Indian Commission, Shaping External Relations in *Time for Action: The Report of the West Indian Commission*, Chapter XI (pages 416 - 459) reveals that the proposal for the establishment of the ACS was made by the Commissioners on the understanding that CARICOM would always act as a group within that body. The proposal would otherwise not have been acceptable to some members of the Commission.

However, since the signing of the Convention establishing the ACS in 1994 the question whether CARICOM is now superfluous has been raised. This is like saying that the OECS is not necessary because all its members are also members of CARICOM.

Experience over the last 14 years has shown that the smaller islands of the Eastern Caribbean need among themselves a very great degree of economic and other forms of integration, common services and functional cooperation, and "the harmonisation of foreign policies" (to use the words of the Treaty of Basseterre which established the OECS). Their proximity to each other is one of the causes of their joint problems (for example, the Law of the sea and bananas) and, consequently, requires many joint approaches and actions. They share a single judiciary and judicial system. They have a common currency and a single central bank. As far as we know, no one has ever asserted that OECS and CARICOM are not compatible or that the OECS is superfluous, given the existence of CARICOM. As everyone knows, they are complementary, not rival, entities.

In fact, while fully committed to the deepening of CARICOM and to membership of the OECS, all the countries of the Windward and Leeward Islands may end up with a political union and nobody could deny that this would clearly be in the interests of the Caribbean Community.

The same argument applies more or less to CARICOM in its relationship with the ACS. CARICOM has a population of approximately 6 million people, and the total population of the ACS is some 200 million. Because of these circumstances, CARICOM and the OECS will always have their indispensable roles to play. Even with the full functioning of the ACS, a CARICOM group approach must be an integral part. Moreover (see Chapter 8), under the FTAA CARICOM will be developing trade and other economic relations with other sub-regional groupings within the ACS. The existence of the ACS will thus facilitate cooperation among the sub-regional groups of CARICOM, CACM, the Andean Group and (through Mexico) with NAFTA.

Given our special features as a sub-region with an identity of its own and seeking to use both the OECS and CARICOM as shields, we should cooperate harmoniously with much more powerful countries and sub-groupings in the western hemisphere.

A good example of a sub-grouping within a much larger economic grouping is Belgium, the Netherlands and Luxembourg (Benelux) within the European Economic Community (EEC) when it was first established in 1958. The three Benelux countries were already in an economic union and after the foundaction of the EEC became even more economically unified. Nobody raised the question whether Benelux would dissolve or fade away with the coming into being of the EEC.

We should not seek to dismantle CARICOM or project its fading away because of the establishment of the ACS. The fact is that we need a deeper and more unified CARICOM to face up to the much vaster ACS. Indeed, the coming into being of the ACS must be accompanied by a deepening of CARICOM and a much more unified stance on matters of foreign policy, including external trade relations.

An English banker who knows the West Indies, the wider Caribbean and Latin America recently stated: "The fact that one or two CARICOM countries are keen on forging new practical trade and economic associations with the wider Caribbean and Latin America does not mean that they should discard existing associations," by which he meant CARICOM.

In dealing with the ACS and other Latin American and Caribbean countries, we must have no illusions. We consist of a group of the smallest and probably the least powerful countries in the hemisphere, so we need what Prime Minister John Compton has called the shield provided by CARICOM so that our West Indian identity and some sovereignty can be enhanced whilst we strengthen our economies through suitable links with the outside world.

Any sensible West Indian knows that the Caribbean Community is not only about trade and economics. It is also very much about intangible factors such as a sense of community, brotherhood and sisterhood, and a strengthened West Indian identity. Even in practical and hard-headed business terms, it would be foolish to give up existing associates in order to have relations with new ones. An important part of the case for CARICOM rests on geo-political and psychological considerations.

CARICOM AND THE EU, CBI, NAFTA/FTAA AND CARIBCAN

We in CARICOM cannot look separately at the EU and NAFTA (FTAA) since, because of our economic structures we need both of them. We have to consider them together if we are to have realistic joint arrangements for our CET and other aspects of external trade policy, and gain remunerative markets for our vital products of bananas, sugar, rum and other agricultural and agro-industrial products and manufactures.

One main reason, apart from continuing market access for sugar, bananas, rum and rice as well as minerals and manufactured goods, is the provision in the Lomé

Convention for non-reciprocity on the part of the African, Caribbean and Pacific (ACP) countries; but should any ACP state provide reciprocity of tariffs to another developed country, this would automatically and immediately entail the extension of identical treatment to products imported from the EU. It is unnecessary to belabour this point, except to emphasise the effects of this on levels of production, foreign exchange earnings, employment and government revenue.

As small and very small countries, we need to diversify geographically our exports and imports and sources of aid and trade. Since the EU is not a single monolithic and dominant organisation, if we wish to have more communication and mutual understanding with it, we should move quickly to establish joint resident CARICOM representation in countries other than the UK, such as France, Germany and Italy. Both the Commission and the member states of the EU have positively and unequivocally encouraged CARICOM (as well as other Caribbean countries not in CARICOM – Suriname, the Dominican Republic and Haiti) to negotiate as a group.

The EU has always strictly adhered to the principle of joint actions towards negotiations involving tariffs and other related matters. It has never even hinted that it is prepared to negotiate individually with the Caribbean countries and has always stressed the need for a joint approach from CARICOM.

CARICOM AND NAFTA/FTAA

There have been some important recent developments in NAFTA in the last 15 months.

1. The US government agreed in early 1994 to give Caribbean Basin beneficiaries parity of treatment with Mexico with regard to textiles and clothing. Exports of clothing to the USA and a few other markets are of great importance to Jamaica.
2. The December 1994 Miami summit of heads of state in the hemisphere agreed to a declaration of principles and plan of action. This document was proposed by both the developed and developing countries of the hemisphere and revealed the problems arising from free trade among countries of greatly unequal levels of development, size, natural and human resources. It drew attention to the need for appropriate transition periods and phasing in of obligations of the less developed and smaller countries and sub-groupings. It noted the need for financial inflows, terms not only for meeting external debt service but also for improving the infrastructure and human resources and for helping the Latin American and Caribbean countries to adjust to both trade liberalisation and the need to build up export-oriented productive investment.

The prime minister of Jamaica, P.J. Patterson, spokesman for CARICOM on extra-regional trade and other economic issues, made a cogent presentation at the Miami summit. He advocated the sub-regional building-block approach and the need for debt relief and for finance generally.

Fundamentally, the Miami summit agreement permits hemispheric free trade to come about either through all Latin American and Caribbean countries and sub-groupings acceding to NAFTA; or by strengthening their existing sub-regional groups and developing free-trade links with each other and including (by inference) the NAFTA sub-grouping. The accession to NAFTA or the sub-regional building blocks approach would end up in the creation of FTAA. It now appears that the preferred approach is the critic of the Free Trade Area of the Americas. This is to be established by the year i this Section, we call the first approach NAFTA and the second approach FTAA, or we just simply say NAFTA (FTAA).

3. In February 1995 Congressman Crane, chairman of the trade sub-committee of the Ways and Means Committee of the US House of Representatives tabled a bill on Caribbean Basin trade security. This proposed extending the CBI for another six years or possibly ten years and including certain hitherto excluded products including, *inter alia*, textiles and clothing, leather and leather products and petroleum products. If this bill becomes law, it will have three great advantages.

- It will give CBI countries six more years of non-reciprocal duty-free entry into the US market.
- It will expire either after six years or when negotiations are completed with NAFTA.
- It will allow time for the sub-regional groupings to strengthen themselves and to develop trade and economic links with each other, including NAFTA.

It appears that the CBI beneficiaries will have the option either to join NAFTA or to have full or partial free trade with NAFTA and other sub-regional groupings. Either would be to the advantage of the CARICOM and CACM countries. In the end each of the regional sub-groupings (CARICOM, CACM, the Andean Group, Mercosur and NAFTA) will have full or partial free trade with each other.

NAFTA is a complex issue. An excellent and balanced analysis of the impact of NAFTA on CARICOM has been recently submitted to the CARICOM Secretariat, carried out by a West Indian team of economists and experts in international trade headed by Frank Rampersad and including among others, DeLisle Worrell. Other important articles on the subject have been written by Richard Bernal, Henry

Gill, Reginald Dumas, Peter King and others, and another study on NAFTA was recently undertaken in the Caribbean office of ECLAC. We should not abandon the parity with Mexico's free access to the US market for certain products which were excluded from free entry into the USA under the CBI. We should also not fail to examine a possible relationship with the proposed South American Free Trade areas (SAFTA) under the FTAA.

All the CARICOM countries have much the same interests in both NAFTA and FTAA, although there are one or two countries which may have a special interest in a few export products. Sugar, rum, rice, bananas, petroleum and natural gas products and some manufactured goods are not produced in every single CARICOM countries. With regard to special exports, the past practice has been for all CARICOM countries to negotiate as a group, with the country or countries producing the product, alongside the CARICOM Secretariat, negotiating as a very small group.

We also all have common interests with respect to not being able to give *complete* tariff reciprocity. To have an interest in one, two or even three products which another CARICOM country has or exports is not a case for individual country negotiations. In Lomé, not all the CARICOM countries produce for export bananas, sugar, rum or rice. In a Preferential Trade Agreement with the USA we also have rum, rice, vegetables and petroleum and natural gas products but we negotiated as one group quite successfully.

CARICOM AND CANADA (CARIBCAN)

Canada is a founder member of NAFTA; CARIBCAN, therefore, may have to be modified, particularly with respect to the non-reciprocal, duty-free access of CARICOM products into Canada. Nevertheless, it is in the interests of the CARICOM countries that other aspects should be negotiated, such as industrial and technical cooperation, particularly in technical education, as well as development finance, both bilateral and through the Caribbean Development Bank (CDB).

Canada, with its good understanding of the problems, needs and aspirations of the West Indian people, and its longstanding but quiet and effective support, both directly and indirectly, in its aid, trade, investment and technical cooperation relationships with CARICOM, can aid the process of closer intra-CARICOM cooperation and integration.

CARICOM should accept the recommendation of the West Indian Commission that it should seek to continue its special relationship with Canada. Moreover, in group negotiations with NAFTA, it can no doubt expect full support from it for its vital interests.

CARICOM's relations with the wider Caribbean and Latin America

CARICOM should negotiate as a group with the EU, CARIBCAN, FTAA, CACM, the Andean Group and Mercosur, in order to further its interests, listed as follows.

1. Continuing the good terms of access for bananas, sugar, rum and rice and all (or nearly all) the extra-regional exports of both commodities and manufactured goods.
2. Preferential (and perhaps reciprocal) duty-free access for all our manufactured exports to both the USA under the CBI and to the EU under the Lomé Convention.
3. Modification of the CARIBCAN agreement so as to include formerly excluded CARICOM products and of the CBI so as to gain access with Mexico to the US market.
4. Access to development aid on concessional terms from the USA, Canada and the EU for physical infrastructure, human resource development and capital inflows for productive sectoral investment.
5. Support for an adaptation and liberalisation fund for specific projects to help improve productivity, lower unit costs and establish new export production.
6. Seeking an increase in the level of private inflows from both blocs, bearing in mind that under the EU and FTAA the Caribbean participants will not merely be CARICOM countries but are likely also to include other countries in the Caribbean archipelago.

CARICOM also has many common interests with the CACM countries in relation to NAFTA and FTAA, provided that the issue of the continuation of our duty-free quota for bananas in the EU vis-à-vis our low-cost competitors of the Central American countries can be settled.

The three lines of action to be taken are:
- diplomacy with the Central and South American exporters of bananas to Europe;
- efforts to advance CARICOM interests with member states of the EU, particularly the UK, Germany, France, the Netherlands and Italy.
- pressing both the EU and the NAFTA for more favourable rules of origin for our manufactured exports to these two markets.

RECIPROCITY IN EXTERNAL TRADE AGREEMENTS

One of the most important issues is reciprocity: the extent to which we should reciprocate by offering duty-free imports from the EU and NAFTA. If we give duty-free entry to the products imported from NAFTA, we will, under the Lomé Convention, have automatically to grant the same concessions to the EU. Such duty-free entry from both these gigantic and highly developed blocs would spell death to CARICOM agricultural and manufacturing sectors, thus depriving our countries of large amounts of foreign exchange and employment. This is essentially why we need transition periods for the maturation of our economies from "adolescent" to "adult" (or more realistically "semi-adult") status. One important distinction should be made here – the commitment to full or nearly full reciprocity combined with a long transition period towards this goal or the exclusion, from the beginning, of many products from duty-free entry for an indefinite period of time.

The issue of reciprocity need not, however, involve an across-the-board arrangement. There could be a large number of exclusions for sensitive products as well as long phasing-in period for others and for some even a lowering of the tariffs rather than a complete removal in respect of these products.

Experience, economic analysis and international justice all combine to require that we not be asked to give total across-the-board duty free entry to products from the two massive groupings of the EU and NAFTA and to a lesser extent, from the bigger Latin American countries. We are highly unequal partners and there is no question of a "level playing-field" existing for all of us. The result is that we will be left defenseless from both a protective and a revenue point of view, and be either marginalised or absorbed. This is a complex matter and we have to prepare ourselves very thoroughly for the negotiations with the blocs or countries concerned.

Also of relevance for weaker partners in a Free Trade Area or closer integration grouping, is access by the weaker partners to financial resources for increasing the capacity to produce competitively exportable products. The case for this is stronger if there are no compensating opportunities for free movement of labour to the stronger partners.

Just as in macroeconomic policy, trade liberalization between highly unequal partners requires "adjustment" on the part of the weaker one, which can only take place if financial resources and technical assistance are transferred from the stronger to the weak and/or if there is freedom of movement of labour.

Reciprocity can also involve giving the developed and bigger partner country or countries the same right to provide services in the less developed and smaller countries on the same terms as nationals of the latter countries or their partners in a close integration grouping. This is an area where there must be a harmonized position among the CARICOM countries. The same issue can be raised with respect to investment, government procurement, etc.

The same degree and scope of reciprocity could also vary as between the MDCs of CARICOM on the one hand and the LDCs on the other hand - that is to say, the OECS countries and Belize. If all CARICOM countries negotiated as a group, this problem would have a better chance of being overcome. Colombia in its Free

Trade Agreement with CARICOM agreed to exempt the CARICOM LDCs from tariff reciprocity.

With regards to direct and portfolio foreign investment, we should take steps to encourage such flows. Foreign portfolio investment would be relatively new in our countries, but the fact is that there are vast amounts of global Insurance and Pension funds which have to be invested either in interest-bearing bonds or in a wider range of venture capital funds for portfolio, and in some cases equity investment, if the project is deemed to be sound enough. A Caribbean Investment Fund which is precisely for venture capital investment is about to be established.

With respect to the European Investment Bank (EIB), we strongly endorse the emergence some years ago of what is termed "quasi-capital" funds – that is, funds whose terms and conditions embody loan as well as equity investment attributes. This operation by the EIB is particularly well suited for National and Regional Development Banks.

A few final observations. First, it appears very likely that we will have to negotiate on these matters with the EU and then with NAFTA (FTAA).

It is important that at an appropriate stage we negotiate a revision of CARIBCAN with Canada. Such a revision should not be confined to trade matters (because Canada is a member of NAFTA) but should also deal with Development Aid, Private Investment, Industrial Cooperation and Technical Assistance, particularly with regard to the development of CARICOM's human resources – including both education of educators and training of trainers. Already as a result of the meeting in Grenada in early March 1996 between the Caribbean Prime Minister and CARICOM Heads of Government, Canada is to support CARICOM in a few very significant areas.

Let us West Indians, ever united to overcome our individual smallness and relative lack of individual power, enter positively into new relationships with our Caribbean and Latin American neighbours on the basis of a Single CARICOM Market and Economy (or an Economic Union) determined to preserve our identity as a West Indian people and to present a unified common front on matters of foreign policy and external trade relations.

Commonsense dictates that CARICOM could become of increasing importance to us while as a united CARICOM we develop relationships with our larger neighbours.

The issue of the relationship between CARICOM and the ACS is really quite simple. If we were shortsighted and thoughtless enough to abandon CARICOM for the ACS, this would mean the end of West Indian unity, identity, self-reliance and self-respect. We would, in the crudest manner, be choosing "marginalisation" or "absorption" instead of "interdependence" or "partnership".

SUGGESTED GUIDELINES FOR A COORDINATED CARICOM EXTERNAL TRADE POLICY

It follows from all we have said in this Chapter that the following suggested guidelines be adopted in terms of our approach to the several external trade policy issues which we urgently face.

(a) Given the specific structural, historical and institutional features of our West Indian economies CARICOM should jointly pursue several "windows of opportunity".

(b) The Conference of CARICOM heads of government should reaffirm their wish to become a group, and at an appropriate time, part of an hemispheric free trade area, as CARICOM needs not only larger markets, but also associated foreign, private investments to develop and export their products – natural resource-based, labour-intensive and skill-based products. Thus, they would forge ahead with their economic stabilisation programmes at full speed and energetically push the debt relief issue with the developed donor countries and international financial institutions. (Where this is relevant, countries should also begin the process of servicing their intra-CARICOM debt).

(c) The route to this could be either accession to NAFTA or *via* the sub-regional building-block approach, ending up with the establishment of substantial free trade links with all the other sub-regional groups in the hemisphere, including NAFTA. This alternative would be the FTAA route.

(d) We should strongly welcome the early passage in 1997 of the Caribbean Basin Trade Security Act, which would give us and the Andean Group continued guaranteed duty-free entry into the US market and broadened access in terms of textiles, garments and petroleum products on a non-reciprocal basis for a six year focus as is our involvement in the FTAA and the EU. In addition we should maintain our special relationship with Canada and if CARICOM enters into a further partial free trade area with NAFTA (or possibly ten-year) period, and which would pave the way for our entrance into either NAFTA or FTAA.

(e) We should agree in principle to also negotiate, as a group, partial or full (but preferably the former) free trade arrangements with the other sub-regional groupings in the hemisphere.

(f) We cannot separate links with the EU from links with North America, and we strongly wish to seek to continue our own very useful Caribbean group relationship with the European Union after 2001, if necessary, on a somewhat modified basis, but still involving trade, industrial cooperation, general technical cooperation, assistance in export promotion, finance on concessional and semi-concessional terms for infrastructure and development of human resources and private capital inflows for directly productive projects in the export sector.

(g) We should clearly state that because of the peculiar structure of our economies, we need continuing links with both North America and Europe.

(h) Because of the highly unequal economic strength between CARICOM and North America, even partial free trade with the latter should entail a less than complete degree of reciprocity in tariffs, provision of services, government procurement, etc. Financing on suitable terms will also be required to reduce the balance-of-payments and revenue impact of trade liberalisation.

(i) CARICOM as a group should develop partial or full free trade areas with CACM, the Andean Group and with Mercosur.

(j) Consideration should be given to the establishment of partial or full free trade agreements with, or associate membership of, CARICOM with other independent countries in the Greater Antilles, who are not yet in any sub-regional grouping.

(k) We intend to use the ACS as an instrument for achieving *inter-alia*, these objectives.

(l) We strongly believe that the ACS is by no means an alternative to, but fully complementary to CARICOM, which, as the smallest set of countries in the pan-Caribbean and the hemisphere, should act as a group within ACS; for CARICOM is the "innermost circle" for us and its further strengthening is vital to us for both economic and non-economic reasons – indeed for our very survival as a West Indian people.

(m) CARICOM, because of its peculiar economic history and current trading structures, needs both North America and Europe and it is very likely that it will negotiate with the latter. (Within the former, CARICOM should seek to maintain a special relationship with Canada). CARICOM also needs some degree of geographical diversity for both exports and imports.

(n) In negotiating all our external trade agreements we should strongly press for non-reciprocity for the LDCs.

PREPARATION AND NEGOTIATIONS

Needless to say, we must start now to prepare for these all-important negotiations. We must systematically collect all the relevant data as a basis for negotiations with the various countries and groups. But, we also need to mobilise all the relevant negotiating skills in the region, including those from the private sector. We need to decide (if only tentatively) on the most appropriate sequencing of negotiation with various sub-groups and with Canada.

10

A Cautiously Optimistic View of the West Indies Over the Next Two Decades

The nature and difficulties of the tasks in front of us are: the continuing increase of production and diversification of production and exports of goods and services; employment creation and alleviation of poverty; human resources development; higher rates of national savings; and greater domestic and regional self-sufficiency in food, are clearly seen by many people in the region. Thus, there will be a very good underpinning for the strenuous efforts we all have to make. There are many opportunities for economic expansion of all the CARICOM countries. West Indians are creative, versatile and innovative. That is why we are optimistic about the future.

Some of the problems are as follows.
1. Little change in the values and attitudes of West Indians, specifically as regards their obligations and rights in relation to the state and to society.
2. The achievement and maintenance of macroeconomic stability in the shortest possible time, together with debt relief and the servicing of intra-regional debt.
3. The achievement of higher levels of savings in order to: finance public infrastructure and private-sector productive investment; increase the local and regional supply of other factors of production in short supply such as large-scale and small-scale entrepreneurship, management and professional, technical and vocational skills.
4. Changes in the international economic and political environment.
5. The extent to which our traditional donor countries and the international financial institutions accept that we need transitional periods with respect to the preferential entry for our exports and a continuing inflow of concessional finance and private funds before we can become more internationally competitive and more self-reliant – the paradox of economic self-reliance.

6. Whether our leaders in politics, the private sector and in NGOs are prepared to put across in non-partisan terms the harsh realities and the disciplined and strenuous internal efforts required for earning our way in the world.
7. The achievement of deepening CARICOM into a single market (or economic union) and a political union among all the OECS countries.
8. The feasibility of a confederation consisting of four separate political entities – the OECS, Barbados, Guyana and Trinidad and Tobago.
9. Using CARICOM as an instrument for increasing our capacity to export to the other countries of the pan-Caribbean, to the rest of the Western Hemisphere, to Europe and to the other world markets.

There are three scenarios open to us, discussed in Chapter 1: marginalisation; absorption; and interdependence or partnership.

Either marginalisation or absorption would have been anathema to West Indian fighters for self-determination and a higher standard of living for the masses, including those now dead: Norman Manley, T. Albert Merryshow, Grantly Adams, Eric Williams, Robert Bradshaw, Forbes Burnham and Errol Barrow. Fortunately, many of those leaders who are still alive feel the same way.

The scenario which is not only desirable but in our view attainable is interdependence with the wider Caribbean, other countries of the Hemisphere, the EU and with the rest of the world, based on unified West Indian internal and external efforts. Much will also depend on our diplomatic and technocratic skills in persuading and in negotiating with large trading blocs, big countries and transnational corporations.

Our attainments as West Indians should not be confined only to cricket, athletics, other forms of sports, intellectual pursuits, the old and new professions, the creative arts and entertainment. Our talents and creative abilities (combined with strenuous efforts) can enable us to earn our way in the world.

Postscript

Just before sending this work to the publisher, I came across a Jamaica newspaper article (*The Sunday Observer*, Jamaica, April 14, 1996) in which David Jessop, an Englishman knowledgeable about the Caribbean, quite openly discussed the handing back by the smaller independent CARICOM countries, grouped in the OECS, of their national sovereignty to the former metropolitan country – the United Kingdom – or to France.

The writer in the same article also referred to a recent proposal by an influential American conservative, Elliot Abrams, in an article entitled "The Shiprider Solution: Policing the Caribbean (*The National Interest*, Washington D.C., Spring 1996) that the independent countries of the Caribbean archipelago (Both CARICOM and non-CARICOM) should hand over responsibility for their "external security" to the United States.

I have warned of the danger of re-colonization of the CARICOM countries for the last decade and a half and I have once again discussed it in this book.

'Absorption' is, in my view, one of three possible alternative future scenarios for the countries of the Caribbean Community.

But mention of this possibility has had very little impact on West Indian readers, to judge from the overwhelming silence on this point.

I infer, rather charitably, that the reason for this lack of reaction is the belief that I have been 'crying wolf' in an alarmist way. Now that all of us can clearly hear the first scratchings of the wolf on the door, we can only hope that the West Indian people and their leaders will become more vigilant about direct and indirect threats to their sovereignty.

Abrams' article, in my view, reflects the arrogance of power and a certain contempt for the West Indian people. He appears to hold us (rather than God or Nature) responsible for our minute size and relative lack of natural resources.

The article is a recitation of a long litany of West Indian woes and shortcomings. We are all small or very small; the only major natural resource, which most of our countries have, is sand (no doubt for tourism); we are overly dependent on external trade preferences and on external aid; our economies are very fragile, vulnerable and internationally uncompetitive; our unemployment rates are alarmingly high; some of our governments are corrupt; we are highly subject to natural disasters; we depend excessively on migration to the USA; we have very limited capacity or indeed inclination to deal with international trafficking in drugs and with 'laundering' of drug money through banks operating locally; we have very limited capability and equipment to safeguard our 'external security'; there is no powerful country close to us to maintain internal and external security, so that the Hemispheric and world superpower will have to carry out this function.

Hence Abrams proposes that in return for extending trade preferences and financial aid to us, the USA should take over responsibility for 'external security' in the independent countries of CARICOM (with the possible exception of Jamaica and Trinidad and Tobago). It is not clear from his text whether he also includes the non-CARICOM independent countries of the Caribbean in this proposal. This means that we ought to have only what the former Soviet Union in 1968 termed 'limited sovereignty', in referring to the other Communist countries of Eastern Europe – the so-called *Brezhnev Doctrine*.

The implications of the article for the West Indies are far-reaching. Negative as it is, it could, paradoxically, have a good consequence in raising our national and regional consciousness. It must make us think about who we are and where we are heading. Moreover, it should lead us to think more deeply than hitherto about our external alignments in the international community, about where our real interests lie and who our real friends are. It should, finally, make us more determined than ever to avoid re-colonization and to retain our West Indian sovereignty and identity.

What can we do to avoid Re-Colonization?

The fundamental question is: What can we do to avoid re-colonization? Some of the measures have already been discussed in the book. At the risk of some repetition, we put forward the following suggestions.

We should seek further to diversify our trading, economic and political relationships across as many continents as possible. However, because of our geographical location and the size and capacity of the United States economy, we will always have significant trade and other economic ties with the USA. It would simply not be possible to effect a substantial reduction of such ties. What we are talking about here is **incremental** diversification for the most part.

The process of constant vigilance referred to earlier must obviously include threats and actions which would severely affect or destroy the basis of our economies, as is now the case with bananas. Putting the point more positively, it goes without saying that successful efforts to strengthen and diversify our economies are a fundamental means of safeguarding and enhancing our independence.

Heightened concern with our sovereignty and our economic survival will lead at both national and CARICOM levels to efforts even greater than hitherto by our political leaders and ministers of Foreign Affairs, National Security, Finance and International Trade to consult with each other on a continuing basis on all matters and issues that appear to threaten our sovereignty - whether of a political, security or economic nature.

It is imperative that our leaders scrupulously avoid our countries being played off against each other by much larger and more powerful neighbouring or distant governments, blocs and private entities.

The expansion of the Caribbean Community (both the Community and the Common Market aspects) must also occupy an important place on our agenda. Eric Williams, once referred to by Errol Barrow as the 'philosopher of Caribbean Integration', always envisaged the economic integration of the entire Caribbean Archipelago irrespective of language and constitutional status of the countries and territories. It is, however, easier to start only with the **independent** and possibly near-independent countries. All the independent countries of the Caribbean Archipelago must, after an initial phase of freer trade through trade liberalization and/or economic cooperation agreements, proceed in the medium-term to come together in a much larger CARICOM Single Market. This would increase our integrated Caribbean Archipelago market from six million to over thirty million people and would obviously greatly enhance our external bargaining-power.

Efforts must also be made by all the Eastern Caribbean members of CARICOM to establish among themselves political union (of varying degrees of closeness ranging from full Federation among some to confederation embracing all), resting on a firm foundation of economic union – although such political union must transcend purely economic matters. The present extent of, and future potential for, political fragmentation in the Eastern Caribbean is simply scandalous and short-sighted on our part and invites both drug trafficking and money-laundering activities, as well as temptation for political interference and the exercise of crude hegemony by more powerful outsiders.

We return here to the question of incrementally diversifying our trade, economic and political relationships with countries other than the world's lone superpower. Here, CARICOM countries should, wherever possible acting as a group, consciously seek to diversify their trade and other external economic and political relations – principally through the Free Trade Area of the Americas (FTAA) proceeding by trade liberalization as between the Hemispheric sub-groupings, starting with the non-CARICOM Caribbean countries, the Central American Common Market, the ANDEAN Group, MERCOSUR and ending up with NAFTA.

We should also view with the utmost interest the attempt now being made to form a South American Free Trade Area (SAFTA), particularly its relationship to the North American Free Trade Area (NAFTA).

In the context of NAFTA, and also outside of it, our economic, diplomatic and political relations with Canada can provide us with some of the contervailing power we need to avoid an extraordinary degree of dominance by the world's only superpower. Canada has no hegemonic ambitions and understands us and our problems better than the superpower. Much the same applies to our economic and political relations with the Association of Caribbean States (ACS) and with the other Latin American countries (save for the misunderstanding of our banana cost and marketing problem by some of these countries).

For the same general reasons, as well as for more specific trade and economic reasons (such as markets for our bananas, sugar, rice, rum, non-traditional agricultural exports and our manufactured goods; financial aid; access to foreign private investment and technology), we should seek to continue and even to intensify our relations with the European Union many of whose member states (and its Commission as well) seem to understand our problems reasonably well. Closer trade and economic relations with East and South-East Asian countries and with India, Pakistan, South Africa and Nigeria also commend themselves.

Diversification of external trade, economic and political relations can be a factor more conducive to a greater degree of effective sovereignty than very close relations with only one or even two superordinate great powers. As the West Indian Commission put it, we now have several 'windows of opportunity' (because of our historical background and our present geo-political situation) and we should make full use of all of them, if only to compensate for our minute size, relative lack of natural resources, and limited individual bargaining power.

There is much to be said in favour of a Federation of all the OECS States (both the Leeward and Windward Islands). The British Virgin Islands and Anguilla should certainly be included as well. This Federation, which would have only one external sovereignty, could become part of a looser Eastern Caribbean Confederation (where, unlike a Federation, individual units retain their separate external sovereignties but agree to exercise them jointly). This Confederation would also include Guyana and Trinidad and Tobago. It would be up to Barbados to decide whether it would form part of the OECS Federation or become a separate unit of the wider Eastern Caribbean Confederation; but this country must obviously be directly included in the one or the other. Suriname could consider becoming a unit of the Confederation at a later stage, after it has fully settled into the CARICOM relationship.

Needless to say, this Confederation, acting wherever possible with their CARICOM partners in the Northern Caribbean, would be vitally concerned with the enhancement of our sovereignty and external security (as well as with our economic and social development, the operation of new Common Services, human rights and good governance). Essentially, it would complement the CARICOM Single Market and Economy agreed for the economic aspect of deepening the Community – the other two aspects of deepening being – (a) Functional Cooperation and Common Services; and (b) the Coordination of Foreign (and External Trade) Policies.

Sovereignty and Psychological Independence

Finally, we discuss a somewhat intangible but most fundamental aspect of the maintenance of our sovereignty – a greater degree of psychological independence. This theme has been dealt with by many twentieth-century West Indian thinkers.

In different disciplines and different contexts, these writers all clearly saw psychological independence as a desirable end in itself as well as a major requirement for achieving and maintaining both formal and effective sovereignty and West Indian identity. Psychological independence, in their view, also entails a certain degree of cultural and intellectual independence. A good example of where we have fallen short in psychological independence is our failure so far to establish the Caribbean Community Court of Appeal with final jurisdiction. The vast majority of other Commonwealth countries – including Canada, India, Pakistan and nearly all the others in Asia and Africa have for some time now had their own Final Appeal Courts. Australia recently announced its intention to do likewise in the near future.

We in the West Indies run the risk of probably being the last set of Commonwealth countries to retain the services of the Judicial Committee of the Privy Council in London.

Another example where somewhat more progress has been made concerns the issue of independence in the form of a monarchy or a republic. Dominica, Guyana and Trinidad and Tobago are now republics and all parties in Jamaica agree that the country should shortly assume republican status under a Presidential Head of State. The others are still monarchies. Obviously whether an independent country of the Commonwealth has the British Queen or a national President as Head of State is irrelevant to the constitutional independence of that country. It is purely a question of national symbolism and psychology.

But national symbols are of great importance. Recently P.J. Patterson, the prime minister of Jamaica, set up a high level National Committee on National Symbols and Observances.

In particular, some measure of intellectual independence is essential in appraising the relevance to the West Indies of the major ideologies of Western European origin – Nationalism (Constructive or Destructive), Political Democracy and Human Rights, Liberal Capitalism, Conservative Capitalism, varying shades of Social Democracy and Democratic Socialism, Communism and Fascism. Some of these go together, others are mutually contradictory. The issue is to what extent should we draw upon Western European ideologies as against indigenous ones?

This brings us to the question of indigenous West Indian thought in the twentieth century. West Indian indigenous thought and writing from a nationalist, democratic and reformist/radical perspective came into full flowering in the twentieth century.[1] It is useful to think of the contributions in terms of three waves:

(a) the first wave, includes writers born before the First World War - people such as Marcus Garvey, C. L. R. James, Philip Sherlock, Eric Williams and Arthur Lewis (born in 1915);

(b) the second wave, includes writers born between the two World Wars. One group – for example, George Lamming, Rex Nettleford, Gordon Rohleher and Edward Kamau Braithwaite (and to some extent and in a different context Vidia Naipaul[2]) grappled directly with the closely related issues of culture, identity and the other psychological aspects of independence. The other was the New World Group with persons such as Lloyd Best, Kari Levitt, George Beckford, Norman Girvan among others. This group was concerned with psychological and intellectual independence as well as with the political economy of West Indian development. (Alister McIntyre made important technical contributions to the subject of Caribbean Development, Caribbean Integration, Monetary Economics and Trade Policy in the early days of the movement).

(c) the third wave, includes those born during and after the Second World War. There are so many that it would be invidious to select only one or two for special mention.

Obviously, these three sets of thinkers differed among themselves and as between their respective waves in terms of the time in which they lived and their experiences, emphases, preoccupations and disciplines. Nor is it a question of one wave replacing another. Each wave leaves a large legacy for succeeding waves in a somewhat cumulative overall process. For example, the following seems to be more or less common to all of three groups:

(i) the achievement and maintenance of West Indian self-determination, the basis of which was seen as full internal self-government (later to be called independence). Garvey was the earliest and C.L R. James the second and most forceful advocate of this;

(ii) the advocacy of more political democracy internally; C.L.R. James was the first to develop this theme of full, unqualified democracy;

(iii) the 'economic emancipation' of the masses, to use Eric Williams' term;

(iv) the need to diversify and strengthen the economic structure; Marcus Garvey, Eric Williams, Arthur Lewis and all in the second and third waves;

(v) greater pride, self-reliance and awareness of their heritage on the part of the masses of African descent. This was strongly emphasised by Marcus Garvey and later on, and continuing up to today, by Philip Sherlock that remarkable West Indian, who in spite of his advanced age, seems to represent all three waves at one and the same time;

(vi) West Indian political unity – most strongly emphasised by C.L.R James, Eric Williams and Arthur Lewis. The hope for Political Union (either of all the West Indian or only the Eastern Caribbean) even after the early demise of the West Indies Federation in 1962 was entertained by Arthur Lewis, Eric Williams and many in the second and third waves. Under the influence of Eric Williams, the New World Group and others of the second wave, favoured economic integration of both the English-speaking Caribbean and the entire Caribbean Archipelago. Michael Manley played an important role in the deepening of CARIFTA into the Caribbean Community (CARICOM) and at the wider Third World level. He also strongly supported Economic Cooperation among developing countries;

(vii) a greater measure of psychological independence emphasized by Garvey, James, Sherlock and Williams. It must be stressed that the sub-topic of intellectual independence emerged most strongly and clearly with the second wave of thinkers, both within and outside the New World Group, examples being: Lloyd Best, George Beckford, Norman Girvan and DeLisle Worrell in the former category and Lamming, Nettleford, Gordon Rohlehr, Edward Kamau Brathwaite in the latter. It is shared by many in the third wave of thinkers such as Hilary Beckles.

One concluding comment on one or two of the leaders of the New World Group. They made the error of unfairly and unjustifiably disparaging the contributions of earlier West Indian thinkers such as Eric Williams and Arthur Lewis. This is most unfortunate – both because of their impiety towards their intellectual ancestors and the conveying of the wrong impression to readers that there was little continuity between previous West Indian writers and the New World Group.

Over the last decade and a half, the third wave has mainly consisted of UWI social scientists and some outstanding West Indian commentators such as Ricky Singh, Tim Hector and Raoul Panton. Suffice it to say that the range of topics is much wider than during the second wave and the number of researchers much larger. Fundamental subjects such as the Environment; Gender Studies; Electoral Behaviour; International Relations; Structural Adjustment; Poverty and the Informal Sector (and many others) are now being given serious attention. On the other hand during the second wave, the main topics were the Political Economy of Caribbean Development; West Indian Integration; the Transnational Corporation; Technology; Race, Class and Colour; Labour Relations; Small Farming; the Labour Market; and Savings. Many of the second wave themes are also being examined by the third wave scholars. But the theme of the Political Economy of Caribbean Development is receiving proportionately less attention than under the second wave.

This increased coverage by the third wave is a healthy and very helpful trend and will certainly accelerate. But we cannot afford to reduce emphasis on the history and theory of long-term development and projections of alternative scenarios.

The concern with the past and future long-term development of the West Indian political economy, with West Indian Integeration and with intellectual independence were the best features in the thought of the New World Group.

This is so not only because we need, as always, a sense of direction but also because of the remarkable progress in Technology and the rapid changes which the world economy is now undergoing as both Owen Arthur, the prime minister of Barbados, and Edwin Carrington, the Secretary General of CARICOM have recently observed. We must 'factor in' these changes in any vision of the future and in any future development models or scenarios which we construct.

There is a rich legacy of ideologies of Western Europe some of which are more universalistic and more humane than others. We cannot avoid adopting the ideals and ideas of these universal and humane systems and concepts already laid down in some of these ideologies. We, however, have to add the 'indigenous factor' to make them ideals and ideas meaningful in our circumstances.

My own view is that we have to draw on the ideals and ideas of some of the West European ideologies and blend them with the dictates of West Indian culture, history, experience and our needs and situation and with the rapidly changing world economic and technological situation. Bearing all this in mind, I would tentatively suggest as a basis for a model (or vision) of economic, social and political development appropriate to our region for the first few decades of the twenty-first century. The following are ten fundamental points:

1. An efficient, diversified and internationally competitive economy in terms of the production of both goods and services and a just and equitable society dedicated to removing poverty and unemployment.
2. The stimulation of a greater measure of pride, self-esteem and self-reliance among all the West Indian peoples.

3. An efficient and, where necessary, economiccally interventionist state operating side by side and co-operatively with an efficient, competently managed and entrepreneurial private sector; and with the state, the private sector and the trade union movement being dedicated to the well-being of all in the nation particularly the well-being of the truly poor and the unemployed.
4. Popular participation in the development process (as distinct from manipulative populism).
5. Recognition of human development (including human resource development as an important element of this as both an end in itself and as a means to national development. Recognition of indigenous West Indian cultural growth and development both as an end in itself and as a means to promoting economic and social development. These two points entail that development should be 'people-centred'.
6. Greater emphasis on the application of Science and Technology (including Information Science and Technology and Biotechnology) to the development of the region by the state, the other social partners and other relevant groups and a prominent role for these areas at all levels of the educational system.
7. Recognition of the fundamental importance of the preservation and improvement of the environment by the state, the other social partners and indeed all persons and entities undertaking physical development and/or construction or engaged in the ownership or operation and maintenance of production facilities, equipment, infrastructure, or residential facilities. Morever, there must be widespread understanding that environmental maintenance and improvement are essential not only for aesthetic, cultural, social and health but also for **economic** reasons.
8. An ideology of psychological, cultural, political and economic Nationalism which emphasises:

    (a) West Indian Unity and Economic integration of the Caribbean Archipelago both as ends in themselves and as means to national development and greater effective sovereignty. This entails respect in all countries for the equality of **all** West Indian people irrespective of economic and social position, race, colour and particular West Indian country of origin. This principle should in future extend to all members of the Caribbean Community to the extent that other Caribbean Archipelago countries become members of the Community.

    (b) active economic, cultural and intellectual interdependence and interaction with the rest of the world (as distinct from the passive dependence which has prevailed for centuries); and

(c) the preservation of our **formal** sovereignty and the maximisation of our **effective** sovereignty.

9. Maintenance and strengthening of political democracy should not necessarily involve any far-reaching amendments of present constitution such as modelling them on the American pattern in situations where Federalism an essential rationale for the American Constitution does not exist. We should also recognise that the excessive seperation of powers in the American model is based on a misunderstanding of the then existing British system by the American Founding Fathers).

   One should not forget that the present constitutions strike an on the whole a sensible balance between speed and reasonable costs in government and parliamentary decision making on the one hand and the public airing of, and deliberations on, political, social and economic issues of the day on the other hand. What may be needed in some countries is the devising of new, or the adaptation of existing, political and economic institutions to facilitate more genuine participation by the grass-roots in the development process. What also seems to be needed is a greater degree of transparency and accountability at all levels of government. In this connection the establishment of more select committee of parliament worth considering, especially when the total numbers in it lower those are not too small. (The issue of retention of the monarchy versus Republicanism is not so much a constitutional question as a matter of symbolism and an assertion of psychological independence).

10. The upholding of Human Rights – political and civil as well as economic, social, and cultural – should be recognised as being of fundamental importance, as is the recognition of the obligations and duties of individuals and groups to the State and the wider Society. Apart from offences against the law being justly and quickly dealt with in an open manner, the grave deficiencies in both the Work Ethic and Business Ethics that now exist must be eliminated by voluntary action of both workers and businessmen at fault.

It can be readily seen that the elements outlined above are rooted in a blend of West European and indigenous West Indian thought, history and experience. Moreover, the relative emphases as between the elements must take into account the ever-changing specific real-world situation in the various countries of the region.

With regard to a special ideological label for this vision, I prefer to be concrete and specific and simply use the term 'a West Indian model (or, if one wishes, ideology) of economic, social and political development'.

But in addition to the adoption of an appropriate model of development, specific concrete programmes of action are required in order to achieve a greater degree of psychological, cultural and intellectual independence. Our leaders and our people at large must seek to:

(i) Generate appropriate national and regional symbols which would inspire and motivate the people.

(ii) Promote better teaching of West Indian and Caribbean History from a Caribbean point of view as compulsory subjects in our educational institutions – primary, secondary and tertiary. In such teaching we need to emphasize our innovativeness and creativity and to stress our achievements in all fields of human endeavours, in spite of the formidable obstacles which we have faced for virtually all our history;

(iii) Continue material and moral support for the activities of the Caribbean News Agency (CANA) and the Caribbean Broadcasting Union (CBU) in projecting West Indian programmes to all parts of the region, and for further efforts to project such programmes to North and South America, Europe and to other parts of the world. There is much to be said in favour of Ian Boxill's proposals for a West Indian radio station and the establishment of a West Indian filmmaking company. More broadly, in culture, creative arts, and electronic mass media, we should make every effort to project abroad what we have produced and not to be content with being passive importers of what emanates from North America and Western Europe. This is one area where more active effort is needed. We should interact with the rest of the world in Culture and the creative Arts, and not be a one-way importer from the dominant centres in the outside world. For example, Jamaica's reggae music in conquering the world is illustrative and inspiring and the same could be done with regard to the calypso and steelband.

Finally, we need more activity in disseminatingting the works of West Indian writers produced by West Indian publishing houses for both the regional and overseas markets.

Our poetry, creative dancing and drama must also be taken to many parts of the world, as is the case with our novels and the Jamaican National Dance Theatre Company.

(iv) To adopt a style of male dress more suitable to our West Indian climate.

(v) To more actively promote indigenous Creative Arts, whether of Afro-West Indian or Indo-West Indian origin or the product of our Creole situation and experience.

(vi) To establish Creative Arts Centres along the lines of the one at UWI, Mona, Jamaica in both the other campus and non-campus territories.

(vii) To make more use of indigenous cultural creations as inputs into the production process and to use such creations as final products for use both within the region and for export to 'niche' markets abroad.

(viii) To promote better informed and a more active and regionally coordinated range of external policies and activities. This requires, *inter alia*, the early establishment of a West Indian 'think-tank'. The region has more than adequate intellectual and technical expertise to create for itself a first class 'think-tank' to deliberate on the major challenges facing us in the region today.

(ix) Judging from present trends, the real gender problem in the West Indies in the next few decades will relate to males rather than to females. Even casual observation today reveals that, particularly at the teen-age level, the young males, compared with the young females, are much less motivated or interested in achievement and seem to be with a sense of purpose and direction. Accordingly, Gender Development Programmes must immediately begin to focus on males as well as females. For, if young males do not become better motivated, they cannot become psychological independent, let alone make an appropriate contribution to economic and social development.

The Problem of Drug Trafficking and Money-Laundering

This has become a major problem in the Caribbean – both mainland and insular. In the CARICOM countries one is increasingly hearing the view that this is a United States problem, since that country is by far the largest consumer of harmful drugs in the world. This view is both short-sighted and morally wrong.

First of all, there is the inevitable spill-over into widespread drug addiction and into major crime and corruption within our West Indian countries. Second, we are members of the international community and should be willing to do whatever we can, within our very limited resources, to assist in the suppression of a trade that causes much human suffering, degradation and a considerable amount of anti-social behaviour in all the consuming countries, world-wide. Obviously, we need a large amount of external support in money, vessels, other equipment and training to make a meaningful effort in severely reducing drug-trafficking in the region. But it must be emphasised again and again that external assistance should not lead us into limiting both our formal and effective sovereignty over our land, our territorial seas and our airspace by treaty or by tacit agreement with external powers.

The approach that seems most consistent with the maintenance of West Indian sovereignty would appear to be the establishment of a CARICOM Anti-Narcotics Programme in which the CARICOM countries as well as USA, UK, Canada,

France and Holland would participate and finance according to their physical capacity number of trained personnel and their ability to pay.

The control of money-laundering must accompany the anti-drug trafficking efforts. This requires utmost care by all governments, Central Banks and commercial banks (acting in co-operation with each other) in legislating for the control of suspect banking transactions and in maintaining day-to-day surveillance over such transactions.

Many of the proposals made above are not new. But their implementation is a matter of great urgency. Any new proposals which I have made have emerged from my acute awareness of the far-reaching implications of the Abrams point of view.

A final observation must be made here. The American authorities are bitterly opposed to the preferential banana regime maintained by the European Union in favour of West Indian banana exports. They seem to overlook the elementary point – already drawn to their attention by some CARICOM heads of government – that the loss of the banana market in Europe would encourage the vigorous expansion of the cultivation of marijuana and the trafficking in cocaine in the islands adversely affected by any termination of the preferential regime.

Some Comments and Reflections on the Abrams Article

Abrams does not see a single redeeming feature in us or in our situation. He overlooks several positive features that we have in spite of our small and very small populations, among them being:

(a) The fact that the CARICOM countries occupy a very high place among the developing countries of the world in the Index of Human Development. The UNDP Human Development Report 1996 (Page 111) presents a new index recently constructed by that organisation to measure human development which takes into account only social development and, unlike previous indexes, leaves out the per capita income factor. Indices were constructed for 101 developing countries. The highest score was made by Chile. Trinidad and Tobago ranked second, Barbados sixth, Jamaica fifteenth and Guyana twenty- fifth. These four countries, which together have some eighty-three (83) percent of the total population of the Caribbean Community, were, very obviously, among the top twenty- five. If Bahamas, Belize, the OECS countries and Suriname were included, CARICOM as a whole would probably rank within the top fifteen to twenty of all developing countries. With regard to other non-CARICOM countries of the Caribbean Archipelago, Cuba ranked tenth and the Dominican Republic sixteenth. Even when per capita income factors are included, the CARICOM countries (including the OECS), rank equally high among developing countries, with Barbados being ahead of

Trinidad and Tobago. In light of this excellent performance in attaining the real goal of economic development, which is 'human' or distinct from 'income' development, how can any reasonable person pour contempt upon the CARICOM countries?

(b) The fact that the vast majority of West Indian countries have good records by Third World and indeed world standards in the upholding of human rights and maintenance of democratic societies.

(c) The fact that most of our political leaders and other politicians are able and articulate and have standards of integrity not significantly below those of the politician in other countries of the world, both developed and developing.

(d) The hard work and determination displayed by many small black farmers growing food crops to feed the local population. In Guyana and Trinidad and Tobago it is mainly small farmers of East Indian origin who have performed this vital role for those countries.

(e) The fact that bananas were introduced in Jamaica towards the end of the 19th century as a black peasant and not a plantation crop to diversify our economies away from total dependence on sugar.

(f) The fortitude, unceasing hard work and determination shown by generations of West Indian mothers in single-handedly bringing up and educating their often numerous children.

(g) The native shrewdness of the average and not necessarily highly educated West Indian which has manifested itself in the quickness with which both manual and technical skills can be acquired and in the enterprise, astuteness and courage of the 'higglers' (most of them females from Jamaica and, to a lesser extent, Guyana) engaging over the last two decades in extensive travelling and trading in both the islands and the mainland countries of the Caribbean.

(h) The fact that many West Indians have risen to very high positions in international organisations and that we have produced some outstanding Civil Servants and diplomats who have served their home countries with distinction. With respect to international organisations, the work of Shridath Ramphal as Secretary-General of the Commonwealth was a landmark of excellence in both vision and diplomacy. He played a most important role in persuading all the Commonwealth Heads of Government to agree on total independence for Zimbabwe and Namibia and on the liberation of the Blacks, Coloured and Indians in South Africa from vicious White domination.

(i) The fact that such a small island as St Lucia (143,000 people) has within the space of just over one decade produced two Nobel Prize Winners – one in Economics and the other in Creative Literature.

(j) Our excellence in the Creative Arts – the novel, drama, poetry, literary criticism, indigenous creative dancing, painting and sculpture. There has also been solid achievement in intellectual work – History and Political Thought; the modern Social Sciences; some aspects of the Natural Sciences; and in the form of the large number of outstanding West Indian academics in American Universities. Nor should we forget other skilled persons and paraprofessionals such as nurses and mechanics of all types at work in that country. In addition West Indians at home have excelled in professional fields as diverse as: Law; Medicine; Surgery, Dentistry; Engineering; Accountancy; Management Science; Consultancy Services; Journalism and the Mass Media; and several other professions, increasingly so in Computer Science.

(k) The fact that there have been, and continue to be, in the USA many black leaders of mass movements, and some persons in very high governmental positions – in both cases of West Indian birth or origin.

(l) The fact that Jamaican Reggae is now a major source of enjoyment for many young people all over the Western World and in Japan; the fact that five decades ago some dispossessed and disadvantaged adolescents and young men from the poorer parts of Port of Spain, Trinidad, with absolutely no formal training in Music, created the steel pan – the only new musical instrument to have been invented in this century. Noteworthy, too, is the fact that they can play with precision and beauty not only the calypso and other forms of West Indian Music but also technically difficult pieces of Classical Music. Finally, the fact that in Trinidad and Tobago and to some extent in Guyana new Afro-Caribbean and Indo-Caribbean musical and dance expressions in a Creolised form have creatively emerged and are very much alive, either separately or in varying degrees of fusion with each other.

(m) The supremacy of the West Indian Team in World Cricket and the achievements of West Indians in world-class and Olympic Athletics (particularly Jamaicans and mainly females) and increasingly in Soccer, Basketball and Netball.

In any balanced assessment of the West Indies and its peoples, the factors listed above must never be omitted, even if our shortcomings (particularly our sometimes less than farsightedness in business and national affairs and our deep-seated tendency to economic and political fragmentation and duplication) are also mentioned.

It is not difficult to paint a very negative picture of any country or group of countries anywhere in the world. But one is truly amazed that an assessment can be so lacking in appreciation of the working, creative, cultural, sporting, intellectual, political, administrative, educational, health, entrepreneurial (small-scale and medium-sized), professional, para-professional and other achievements of the West Indian people and Governments. And this, in the face of a history of the plantation system, slavery, indentureship, other forms and degrees of cultural and psychological uprooting and violence, centuries of political and economic colonialism (the latter only recently terminated). The student of Caribbean affairs and Caribbean history, in most cases, today tends to give a better balanced, account of our small part of the world. But perhaps it is too much to expect objectivity and balance from those who are primarily concerned with their perceptions of their own national security interests.

Small as we may be, we have much more to offer the World Community and World Civilization than could be expected, on the basis of statistical probability alone, from a group of six million people with such an unpropitious historical and psychological background.

I am confident that in the years to come, the Hemisphere and the world at large will recognize us as a people of value and of high achievement in very many fields of human endeavour while at the same time, partly through greater self-reliance and international competitiveness, we improve our economies and considerably reduce poverty and unemployment in our midst.

The Continuing Relevance and Necessity of CARICOM, A Single Market and Single Economy

Two articles recently written by a well-known West Indian economist were drawn to my attention after the manuscript of this book had been sent to the publisher. One article entitled 'New Vistas for a Caribbean Community' appeared in CARICOM Perspectives in a Souvenir Issue, June 1995. The other Note was submitted in the form of a Government memorandum in the early part of 1996.

The writers' argument was very simple. Since the whole world is rapidly heading towards globalization of production and towards free trade in goods and services, free movement of capital (and all levels of labour?) and financial, monetary, interest rate, exchange rate and other forms of liberalization, the need for regional free trade and sub-regional integration groupings has greatly diminished and may even disappear. The writer of the Notes argues that, under these circumstances, a Single Market and Economy for the Caribbean Community becomes totally irrelevant. In other words, if the entire world economy were soon to become a single economic space, why should we concern ourselves with regional and sub-regional trade and economic groupings such as the CARICOM Single Market or, for that matter, CARICOM itself or – we may add – the European Union or MERCOSUR or even with the present NAFTA?

The implicit assumption made by the writer is that, in the not too distant future, the entire world economy will be completely freed up, because of the operation of the World Trade Organization (WTO) and because of the move towards hemispheric and global liberalization. He seems to envisage the complete elimination of tariffs and other barriers to free trade, free movement of all forms of capital (and all levels of labour skills?), the free movement of services, the right of establishment in every country by persons and firms from virtually all the countries of the world and the right of procurement by a national of any country of the world for public sector goods and services in all other countries. This would render trade and economic groupings such as CARICOM totally irrelevant and unnecessary.

I have never claimed to be a prophet but I would be surprised if the result of the operations of WTO, of the coming into being of the Free Trade Area of the Americas (FTAA) and an association with the European Union would result in total and full reciprocal free trade and other aspects of economic liberalization for all the CARICOM countries. Whatever neo-liberal economists may say, there cannot and ought not to be full and total reciprocity across-the-board between small and relatively less developed countries and bigger and more developed countries and trading blocs comprised of such countries.

Clearly, even neo-liberal economists admit that there will have to be transition periods for the phasing in of certain aspects of reciprocity. But at the end of a set of transi-tion periods both economic analysis and equity dictate that we could not and should not grant complete reciprocity in trade in all goods and services and in all other economic transactions. To illustrate: in tariff policy, reciprocity should and does not mean that at the end of the transition period all tariffs imposed by CARICOM countries on goods from NAFTA, the other countries of the FTAA and the European Union must be zero. This would be totally impractical and would virtually destroy the economies of the countries of the Caribbean Community. Already there has been truly massive reduction of protection in Guyana, Jamaica and Trinidad and Tobago. This is the combined result of the sudden and rapid removal of quantitative restrictions and the process of phasing down of the Common External Tariff to a maximum protective rate of 20 percent as part of Structural Adjustment Programmes.

How much scope can there realistically be for further reduction of protection for goods imported from NAFTA and the European Union?

In practice, reciprocity in limited areas may have to be granted, but there can be no question of total economic disarmament in a hostile and vastly unequal world. This could only be the result of less than skilful negotiations on the part of the CARICOM countries. The length of the transition period would vary from area to area and item to item but even at the end of the various transitional periods, we could not completely liberalize all trade in goods and services and all other economic transactions.

In some very sensitive sectors and sub-sectors and for certain non-trade transactions there could well be no movement whatsoever of certain economic and trade instruments such as tariffs. It is sometimes claimed by international financial institutions that CARICOM has been too 'inward-looking' and autarchic. This is by no means the case. The Common Market Annex to the Treaty of Chaguaramas certainly does not envisage any substantial degree of trade and other forms of economic autarchy in the CARICOM economic integration process. Article 46 (e) of the Common Market Annex to the Treaty of Chaguaramas provides that a major objective of the industrial policy of CARICOM is 'the promotion of exports to markets both within and outside of the Common Market'.

The future external commercial policy of CARICOM as it is transformed into a Single Market and Economic Union can best be described as one of 'Open Regionalism', as it has been so aptly put by the United Nations Economic Commission for Latin America and the Caribbean (ECLAC).

This is a somewhat complex concept but an important aspect of it is that there would still be scope for some degree of regional or sub-regional import substitution but that much greater emphasis must be placed in future on greater international competitiveness and on the active promotion of exports to third countries. In other words, developing regional and sub-regional groupings in Latin America and the Caribbean must move to a position somewhere between a high degree of self-sufficiency and full opening up of their economies to the world; but this does not by any means imply **full** and **total** integration into the world economy, which would become a single economic space. Moreover, in future our participation in the world economy must be less passive and dependent and more active and entrepreneurial than it has been over the last three and a half centuries.

In addition, if at some point in the medium-term future the three large independent countries in the Greater Antilles not yet members of any close sub-regional economic grouping (with a total population of over twenty-five million people), were to become members of CARICOM, this would increase the size of the CARICOM Single Market from six to more than thirty million people.

The writer also argues that harmonization or even convergence of macro-economic policies would be difficult to achieve because at present the CARICOM economies tend to be more integrated with outside countries than with each other. But even though the OECS countries are more closely linked to outside countries than to each other, this does not prevent them from having a common currency, a common pool of foreign exchange reserves and a common exchange rate. Moreover, the harmonization of interest rates, monetary policies and rates of inflation could be achieved by removing the national barriers which tend to segment money and capital markets. Nor is there anything to prevent them in the future from developing a broadly similar fiscal policy. This would be greatly assisted by the fact that the Eastern Caribbean Central Bank is legally (and probably politically) unable to finance any sizeable fiscal deficit in any member country. In any event, both the OECS (and CARICOM) countries all have similar interests in developing sound macro-economic policies.

A major and beneficial by-product of harmonization or convergence of macro-economic policies as between CARICOM member states would be the imposition of always desirable macro-economic discipline on all the countries. Such discipline would significantly contribute to the decrease in inflation and uncertainty and an increase in investment, production and international competitiveness in our economies.

This would increase both intra-regional trade and extra-regional exports. Nor should we neglect to aim at the benefits of the compatibility as between member-states of policies and programmes in the productive sectors.

One may argue that the formation of large continental (or very large region-wide) trade blocs and of smaller but closer sub-regional integration groupings can move the world closer to liberalization of trade in goods and services, other aspects of world economic integration and indeed to a single world economic space. But this conclusion would depend on three conditions:

(a) that the newly established WTO and full adherence by the Contracting Parties to the commitments undertaken under the Uruguay Round are fully effective in moving the **whole** world and its constituent **individual** countries forward towards free trade in goods and services and other aspects of world economic integration;

(b) that all barriers to trade in goods and services and other economic transactions with third countries put up by nation-states and regional and sub-regional groupings will on the whole be very low or non-existent and where they do exist, highly 'transparent'. Or, to put the point differently, that the very large regional trade blocs and the smaller but tighter sub-regional economic groupings are not overly 'inward-looking' but are characterised by an extraordinarily high degree of 'open regionalism'; and

(c) that there is not only free trade in goods and services but also **completely** free movement of all forms of capital and all levels of labour skills throughout all countries of the world.

We believe that all these conditions are crucial and that the forces of 'economic nationalism' at the national, sub-regional, regional and world level will still continue to operate – although in a somewhat more liberal and outward-looking manner than before. In many of the developing countries, 'trade diversion' and 'protection', while not as excessive as previously, will continue to be seen as aids to development rather than in 'static welfare' terms.

No one can reasonably expect that in the twenty-first century the whole world economy will become one single fully integrated economic unit, (that is, a single economic space), even though the world is likely to be more liberal in trade and other economic transactions than in the period between 1960 and 1990. But even if full and total global integration is ever achieved, it will raise in an acute form the intractable and probably insoluble issues of: (a) fully democratic, participatory and powerful World Government; or (b) as very much a second best – a much more democratic participatory and powerful trade, financial and economic role for the developing countries in the UN, its Organs and Specialised Agencies, (including the two Bretton Woods financial institutions); or (c) a severe and intolerable reduction in the degree of national sovereignty of smaller and relatively less developed countries, which would probably be unacceptable to such countries.

In other words, it is highly unlikely that in the next century, the world will become a single economic space. If this turns out to be the case, there will still be room for nation-states, political unions of such entities, deep sub-regional integration groupings and, at the continent-wide (or large region-wide) levels, regional Free Trade Area (or, as in the special case of Europe, regional integration of considerable depth and scope).[3]

In some cases the sub-regional groupings of Third World countries would have only partly reciprocal free trade arrangements with larger regional groupings of developed countries and with each other. Nevertheless the world economy will still be far from completely globalized, liberalized and fully economically integrated. In other words, there would be room for the European Union, the LOME Convention (or its successor), NAFTA, probably a SAFTA, the FTAA, a widened CARICOM Single Market, MERCOSUR, the ANDEAN Group, the Central American Common Market and other sub-regional and regional groupings in Asia, Africa, the Indian Ocean and the Pacific.

Indeed, the likelihood is for a strengthening of the tendency towards sub-regional groupings among third world countries functioning within the framework of wider Region-wide or continent-wide trade liberalisation groupings,[4] with membership of not a few developed countries. What is more, most nation-states are likely to survive, except where, partly through their own fault in failing to develop a much greater degree of international competitiveness and/or failure to develop deep sub-regional economic and, in some cases, political integration links with similar neighbouring countries, they are 'absorbed' or their national sovereignty severely limited and possibly terminated by a neighbouring or even fairly distant hegemonic power.

Finally, the writer of the two Notes being discussed here argues for the Political Union of the English-speaking Caribbean (or, if we may interject a more realistic note here, such countries in the Eastern Caribbean). This is obviously a laudable goal.

But if there is no CARICOM Single Market and other arrange-ments for achieving Economic Union, it is difficult to see any realistic basis for Eastern Caribbean Political Union. For a Political Union, like a nation-state, has to be based on a single economic space.

This remains the case even though the arguments for such a Union transcend purely economic considerations and include the benefits of a unified and more effective foreign policy and external Security arrangements; good governance; respect for human rights; the establishment of more cost-effective Common Services in Public Administration, Human Resource Development, Science and Technology, Telecommunications, Tax Assessment and Collections, Government Audit, Statistics etc; as well as a firmer basis for the strengthening of West Indian cultural identity and sense of kinship.

Therefore, to have West Indian Political Union without an underpinning of Economic Union would be like talking about Hamlet without referring to the Prince of Denmark. Or, to put it another way, it would be like the grin of the Cheshire Cat – a grin but no cat!

The CARICOM and Extra-CARICOM Markets

It is now clear to all concerned that the desired progress in the agro-industrial and manufacturing sector of CARICOM member states depends on a CARICOM with no impediment to free and fair intra-regional trade as well as on access (and entry) into extra-CARICOM markets. The reason is obvious and has to do with the size of the CARICOM market. To say this is not to disparage CARICOM. We all knew from the very beginning that CARIFTA (succeeded by CARICOM) was only a first step in the quest for external markets for the agro-industrial and manufacturing sectors. (This obviously does not mean that the Caribbean Common Market, or the proposed Caribbean Single Market, is unimportant or useless as a set of instruments for trade and economic integration and development or that the other fundamental and vital aspects of the Caribbean Community (such as Common Services and Functional Corporation and Coordination of Foreign Policies) should be played down.

Apart from better machinery for surveillance, sanctions and dispute settlement regarding unfair trade practices in CARICOM, there are four ways of emerging from this limited market situation and getting substantial access (and entry) into wider markets.

First, we must in the medium term widen CARICOM to include other independent countries of the Caribbean archipelago as members of CARICOM. Second, we must seek to negotiate develop, on a CARICOM basis, free trade arrangements and other relationships of economic co-operation with Latin America (including the mainland Caribbean countries), Canada and the USA – all within the framework of the FTAA. Already we are doing precisely this on a CARICOM basis. But we as a CARICOM group should follow keenly, developments with regard to the proposed South American Free Trade Area (SAFTA). Third, in relation to the USA specifically, we should lobby for the enactment of the Bill to extend to the beneficiary countries of CBI (Central America and the Caribbean) parity with Mexico for certain products which we, the CBI beneficiaries, are now precluded from exporting to the USA, largely because Mexico, unlike the CBI countries, has free access to the US market for these products. Fourth, we ourselves in CARICOM must produce, refine and introduce a strong set of macro-economic policies and sectorial policies and programmes, strongly supported by the Governments and the other social partners, to make our economies more internationally competitive.

I have always held the view that we in CARICOM must make every effort to become internationally competitive. I differ from the neo-liberal economists only in the **speed and scope** of the process of our becoming internationally competitive and of the extent of our opening up of our other economic transactions with the outside world. If in the end we do not achieve international competitiveness, we will not survive economically (and, for that matter as politically independent units).

The heads of government of all the CARICOM countries are now acutely aware of the need to seek access (and entry) into non-CARICOM markets in the Caribbean archipelago and the South and Central American mainland – no doubt with the degree of reciprocity being a central issue in the negotiations.

It should be borne in mind that the issue of full or partial trade reciprocity will arise in the negotiations on these initiatives. To the extent that we have to grant reciprocity, this would once again emphasise the need for us to become more internationally competitive as soon as is practicable. For we have to be competitive to take advantage of free trade opportunities as well as to stand up to free entry of products into our own markets when we give a large degree of reciprocity.

One or two brief points concerning intra-regional trade in goods, services and other invisibles are worth making here. When one looks at intra-regional statistics of trade in goods, one sees that a particular member country of CARICOM is dominating this trade, even when one excludes its exports of petroleum products.

But one needs more than data on trade in goods to draw firm conclusions on the sharing of the benefits of economic integration. Given the orientation of many of our economies towards services (mainly tourism) we must also look at data on 'intra-regional trade' in services (mainly tourism) and in other invisibles such as emigrants' remittances; management, licensing and franchising fees; royalties; consultancy services' fees; profits on Construction contracts; insurance premia; flows of interest, dividends and, where relevant, interest on private capital flows, etc. We must also look at all forms and servicing of intra-CARICOM public aid flows and their servicing, including re-scheduling and even write-offs of principal repayments and interest due on intra-CARICOM debt. Only in this way will one get an accurate measure of relative gains and losses from intra-CARICOM economic transactions. The fact that one CARICOM country is increasing its favourable trade balance in intra-regional visible trade has lessons for all CARICOM countries. First, it shows that CARICOM countries can become more internationally competitive in agro-industrial and manufacture goods. Second, the country that is becoming more internationally competitive within CARICOM has to go further and become more competitive vis-à-vis other Latin American and non-CARICOM Caribbean countries, with the present NAFTA countries and indeed with the member states of the European Union. Third, the country concerned must be ever vigilant about both increasing and **maintaining** its present degree of competitiveness; for, as Caribbean economic history shows, it is possible for countries to slide back in this regard. There is no room for complacency and resting on one's oars. Continuing effort is the name of the game.

Finally, the other CARICOM countries must learn from experience and seek to emulate and even overtake the country that has so far done relatively well in intra-CARICOM trade. For , if the other countries cannot successfully compete with another CARICOM country, how could they possibly hope to compete with many of the other countries in Latin America, the wider Caribbean, NAFTA and the European Union, particularly in light of the fact that they may have to give some degree of tariff reciprocity in forthcoming negotiations for trade and association agreements with these countries and trading blocs? The present intra-regional trade situation should further stimulate **all** CARICOM countries to initiate and/or accelerate concrete action programmes to become more internationally competitive as soon as is economically and socially practicable.

NOTES

1. This Section refers only to the work of writers. It does not look at political or Trade Union activists except where they have written and published.
2. See Naipaul's novel *The Mimic Men*

3. The European Union is exceptional in that, although it is a large Continent-wide grouping, it has gone further than any other (among both developed and developing countries) in achieving and expecting a very deep from and wide scope of integration.
4. The European Union, as a deeply integrated grouping, would be somewhat of an exception, in that it would have non-reciprocal or possibly only partially reciprocal free trade arrangements with groups of developing countries.

APPENDIX A

Grand Anse Declaration and Work Programme for the Advancement of the Integration Movement

Issued at the Tenth Meeting of the Conference of Heads of Government of the Caribbean Community, Grand Anse, Grenada, July 1989.

At this our Tenth Meeting here in Grenada, we, the Heads of Government of the Caribbean Community inspired by the spirit of cooperation and solidarity among us are moved by the need to work expeditiously together to deepen the integration process and strengthen the Caribbean Community in all of its dimensions, to respond to the challenges and opportunities presented by the changes in the global economy. Accordingly, we set out a work programme and specific initiatives to be implemented over the next four years.

THE COMMON MARKET

We are determined to work towards the establishment, in the shortest possible time, of a single market and economy for the Caribbean Community. To that end, we shall ensure that the following steps are taken not later than 4 July 1993, taking into account the need for the continuance of Special Measures for the LDCs:

1. The three Common Market Instruments required by the Treaty of Chaguaramas – the Common External Tariff, the Rules of Origin, and a Harmonized Scheme of Fiscal Incentives – fully revised, agreed and effective by January 1991;
2. Customs cooperation and our Customs Administrations strengthened to prepare ourselves for movement towards a Customs Union;
3. The signature by all of us to the Agreement establishing CIPS by September 30, 1989;
4. The enactment, by January, 1990 of the legislation required to give effect to CIPS and the CARICOM Enterprise Regime (CER);

5. A scheme for the movement of capital introduced by 1993 starting with the cross-listing and trading of securities on existing stock exchanges;
6. Technical work to commence immediately on the establishment of a regional Equity/ Venture Capital Fund;
7. The CARICOM Multilateral Clearing Facility strengthened and re-established for current and capital transactions by December 1990;
8. Further arrangements for intensifying consultation, cooperation on monetary, financial and exchange rate policies by July 1990;
9. The removal of all remaining barriers to trade by July 1991;
10. Immediate activation of Article 39 of the Treaty of Chaguaramas in order to promote consultation, cooperation and coordination of policies at the macro-economic, sectoral and project levels;
11. Arrangements by January, 1991 for the free movement of skilled and professional personnel as well as for contract workers on a seasonal or project basis;
12. Immediate and continuing action to develop, by 4 July 1992, a regional system of air and sea transportation including the pooling of resources by existing air and sea carriers conscious that such a system is indispensable to the development of a Single Market and Community;
13. Greater collective effort for joint representation in international economic negotiations and the sharing of facilities and offices to this end, with immediate effect.

DEVELOPMENT ISSUES

In examining the longer term prospects for development, we recognize the primary importance of Human Resource Development and the expansion of scientific and technological capability to the modernization of the regional economy.

Accordingly, we adopted the resolution in Annex 1 on Human Resource Development and the University of the West Indies (UWI) which among other things recognizes the pivotal role of the UWI and enshrines our commitment that it shall continue indefinitely as a regional institution.

Human Resource Development is of special value in the exploitation of new opportunities arising in the services sector through the development of information technology. We consider these possibilities to hold significant potential for economic growth and development. Accordingly, we should initiate immediately, consultations with the private sector, trade unions and educational institutions to determine the specific strategies for taking full advantage of these opportunities.

We are conscious that people, rather than institutions, are the creators and producers of development. We acknowledge the special roles of the private sector, the trade union movement, the regional universities, the religious organizations, women and youth organizations and people of all walks and conditions of life in moving CARICOM forward.

In this connection, we agree to take the following steps:

(i) The establishment of an Assembly of Caribbean Community Parliamentarians and of a Ministerial group to work out the modalities;

(ii) The establishment of an Independent West Indian Commission for Advancing the Goals of the Treaty of Chaguaramas as agreed in the resolution at Annex II;

(iii) The convening of a Caribbean economic conference as agreed in the Resolution at Annex III;

(iv) The elimination, by December 1990, of the requirement for passports for CARICOM nationals travelling to other CARICOM countries;

(v) The elimination of the requirement for work permits for CARICOM nationals beginning with the visual and performing arts, sports and the media travelling to CARICOM countries for specific regional events;

(vi) The organising of a series of events around 1992 to highlight our achievements in the areas of sports, the performing arts, literature and other areas of cultural endeavor, business and commerce and education. The series will commence with the staging of CARIFESTA in 1991 and include a major Trade fair early in 1992 in Trinidad and Tobago.

We are acutely aware of the fragility of the environment on which our economies rest and of the myriad threats to that environment from internal and external actions and activities. To protect our environment, we support all international initiatives to safeguard the global environment and strongly endorse the Port of Spain Accord on the Management and Conservation of the Caribbean Environment by our own Ministers responsible for conservation of the Environment.

MACHINERY FOR INTER-GOVERNMENTAL CONSULTATIONS

In order to ensure the full and timely implementation of the programme set out above, we shall intensify and make more frequent the contact and consultations among ourselves. We shall meet as often as necessary to advance the decision making and the implementation of this programme.

APPENDIX B

Statistical Tables on Economies of the Caribbean Community and the Wider Caribbean

TABLE 1A
SOME BASIC STATISTICS OF THE CARICOM COUNTRIES

CARICOM Countries	Area (km^2)	Estimate of mid-year population ('000)	GDP per head (US$)	Imports (US$ mn)	Exports (US$ mn)
Guyana	214,970	754.4	340	310.9	268.1
Belize	22,960	184.9	1,973	211.3	129.0
Bahamas	13,039	253.3	11,096	-	-
Jamaica	11,424	2,403.5	1,662	1,877.1	1,156.9
Trinidad & Tobago	5,128	1,227.4	4,050	1,261.6	2,080.5
Dominica	750	83.5	2,050	117.9	54.9
St Lucia	616	151.3	2,415	271.3	127.3
Antigua and Barbuda	442	84.0	4,985	230.7	16.7
Barbados	431	257.4	6,645	700.0	209.4
St Vincent & the Grenadines	388	118.0	1,620	136.1	82.7
Grenada	345	100.2	2,000	109.5	26.6
St Kitts & Nevis	269	42.9	3,656	102.0	19.0
Suriname	1990	422	7,250.0	374.4	465.9
Montserrat	103	12.0	6,133	34.7	1.7

SOURCES: West Indian Commission, *Statistical Profile of the Caribbean Community*, 1992.
UN/ECLAC, *Statistical Yearbook for Latin America and the Caribbean*, 1992.

TABLE 1B
BASIC STATISTICS ON SOME NON-CARICOM ACS COUNTRIES

Non-CARICOM countries	Total population mid-year ('000)	GDP per head (US$)	Imports (US$ mn)	Exports (US$ mn)
Honduras	5,299	608.9	863.5	616.7
Nicaragua	3,808	468.9	688.0	265.8
El Salvador	5,279	676.6	1,294.1	363.3
Guatemala	9,467	925.5	1,673.0	1,202.1
Costa Rica	3,113	1,441.8	1,697.8	1,490.5
Colombia	32,862	1,447.3	4,535.0	7,268.5
Venezuela	19,753	3,580.0	10,101.0	n/a
Mexico	86,309	2,483.0	38,184.0	n/a
Panama	2,466	1,640.1	4,981.0	n/a
Haiti	6,619	199.0	300.4	162.9
Dominican Republic	7,320	1,056.2	1,728.8	658.3

SOURCE: UN/ECLAC, *Statistical Yearbook for Latin America and the Caribbean*, 1992.

TABLE 1C
BASIC STATISTICS

Non-CARICOM countries	Total population mid-year ('000)	GDP per head (Pesos)	Imports (Pesos)	Exports (Pesos mn)
Cuba 1989		2,590.9	2,824.2	5,392.0

SOURCE: UN/ECLAC, *Statistical Yearbook for Latin America and the Caribbean*, 1992; UN/ECLAC, *Agricultural Statistics*, Vols. X and XI, 1993.

TABLE 1D
BASIC STATISTICS

Non-CARICOM countries	Total population year-end ('000)	GDP per head	Imports (NAF mn)	Exports (NAF mn)
Netherland Antilles	191,311	n/a	3,891.0	2,862.0

SOURCE: Source: Netherlands Antilles, *Statistical Quarterly Bulletin* No.14, 1993.
NOTE: Exchange rate US$1.00 = NAF 1.78.

TABLE 1E
BASIC STATISTICS

Non-CARICOM countries	Total population mid 1991 ('000)	Area ('000 km^2)	GDP per head (US$) 1991
Netherland Antilles	192	1	>10,000
Martinique	363	1	>2,500
Guadeloupe	395	2	<10,000
Suriname	457	163	3,630

SOURCE: World Bank, *World Development Report*, 1993.

TABLE 1F
BASIC STATISTICS

Non-CARICOM countries	Total population mid 1991 ('000)	Area ('000 km²)	GDP per head (US$) 1991
Haiti	6.6	28	370
Dominican Republic	7.2	49	940
Cuba	107.36	111	na.
Mexico	83.3	1,958	3,030
Colombia	32.8	1,139	1,260
Venezuela	19.8	912	2,730
Panama	2.5	77	2,130
Honduras	5.3	112	580
Nicaragua	3.8	130	460
Guatemala	9.5	109	930
Costa Rica	3.1	51	1,850
El Salvador	5.3	21	1,080

SOURCE: World Bank, *World Development Report*, 1993.

TABLE 1G
BASIC STATISTICS

CARICOM countries	CARICOM imports as % of total imports	CARICOM exports as % of total exports
Guyana	n.a.	6.1
Bahamas	n.a.	n.a.
Jamaica	4.7	6.2
Trinidad & Tobago	6.2	13.1
Dominica	21.3	25.2
St Lucia	17.9	18.1
Antigua & Barbuda	10.9	66.4
Barbados	15.5	31.3
St Vincent & The Grenadnes	20.8	31.6
Grenada	23.5	22.6
St Kitts & Nevis	15.1	18.3
Montserrat	15.6	33.8
Belize	6.2	8.0

SOURCE: West Indian Commission, *Statistical Profile of CARICOM*, 1992.

TABLE 2A
VALUE OF TOTAL EXPORTS BY CARICOM COUNTRIES TO ALL DESTINATIONS, 1980 - 1994 (EC$'000)

CARICOM Countries	1980	1981	1982	1983	1984	1985	1986	1987	1988	1989	1990	1991	1992	1993	1994
CARICOM	16002004	15123885	12407472	10471953	10265396	9609630	754165	7853890	8369995	9390682	11094806	10900437	10645571	10174290	10744186
MIDCs	15511590	14310581	11789811	9776820	9511331	8855077	6573380	6869384	7135643	8233711	9826474	9707312	9362790	8901540	9634242
Barbados	617766	625941	6833199	968530	1062951	955507	745582	435356	478162	505522	580716	559904	513371	491375	487639
Guyana	1052166	945098	697984	509368	553018	547640	509309	572797	556280	723439	501912	684956	960909	1106193	-
Jamaica	2612064	2637298	2077883	1962790	2027136	1532866	1577031	1912752	2250505	2745857	3123498	3106966	2844698	2903511	3292646
Trinidad & Tobago	11029594	10162721	8330625	6336132	5868226	5819064	3741458	3948479	3850696	4258893	5620348	5355486	5043812	4400461	6053957
LDCs	690414	753827	617660	695135	754065	754553	968485	984506	1234352	1156971	1270332	1193145	1282781	1272750	909944
Belize	298704	294380	244329	209893	251646	243383	250128	277682	313906	334931	348432	321178	367036	340830	385828
OECs	391710	458447	373331	485240	502419	511170	718357	706824	920446	822040	921900	871967	915745	931920	5224116
Antigua & Barbuda	84285	107607	-	59360	47495	-	52876	52549	49641	46481	56152	108137	147599	197567	-
Dominica	26302	51755	66009	74171	69226	75766	117405	129745	149993	121855	148586	146455	144351	129631	122598
Grenada	46946	51356	50087	49539	49114	60333	77776	85234	88908	75568	70771	62623	-	53348	-
Montserrat	3199	5965	6998	12333	8512	7824	6117	9515	6241	4309	4708	2733	4258	6126	7851
St. Kitts & Nevis	65131	65506	50856	49746	54399	55011	67904	75575	74102	77246	74656	74200	70624	66162	-
St. Lucia	124190	111312	112326	128268	129051	140473	223927	214738	321382	295146	343679	296601	335950	322972	256096
St. Vincent & the Grenadines	41657	64946	87055	111823	144622	170763	172352	139468	230179	201435	223348	181218	212963	156114	137571

SOURCE: CARICOM Secretariat

TABLE 2B
VALUE OF TOTAL IMPORTS BY CARICOM COUNTRIES FROM ALL SOURCES, 1980-1994

CARICOM Countries	1980	1981	1982	1983	1984	1985	1986	1987	1988	1989	1990	1991	1992	1993	1994
CARICOM	15895568	16931583	17646885	14863024	12424330	11286909	10627897	10981318	11783279	13785504	14276464	1537460	13984088	15883165	14703905
MDCs	14328360	15135681	15978112	13321055	10694510	9427007	8483542	8469744	8967496	10686972	10974485	11822235	10846391	12448727	12171549
Barbados	1445304	1573978	1493894	1686113	1788293	1649134	1594451	1398453	1571239	1828352	1900690	1886921	1415418	1557740	1658544
Guyana	1070245	1199394	756398	664430	567886	609476	576278	448154	475919	662107	595279	555607	989253	1232397	1117205
Jamaica	3190037	3987519	3739669	4005796	3156683	3011874	2607916	3332537	3873342	4937428	5068296	4858600	4570467	5910957	5878406
Trinidad & Tobago	8622974	8394710	9988151	6964716	5181648	4146523	3704897	3290600	3046996	3299085	3410220	4521107	3871253	3747633	3517394
LDCs	1667008	1775982	1668693	1541969	1730020	1869902	2144355	2511574	2816083	3098532	3301979	3345225	3137697	343438	2532356
Belize	404337	437311	345600	301835	351504	346050	329409	386103	488631	582378	570370	691678	739877	758464	701843
OECs	1262671	1338671	1323093	1240134	1378516	1523852	1814946	2125471	2327452	2516154	2731609	2853547	2397820	2675974	1830513
Antigua & Barbuda	343394	371965	374894	294059	356113	447893	559885	676069	591987	513711	600482	664006	577963	542096	
Dominica	128730	134104	128191	121710	156104	149376	150687	179216	236334	289099	318392	295978	284693	253225	259139
Grenada	135574	146710	152429	154479	151096	186997	225537	239221	248842	272319	294150	316525	-	338754	322430
Montserrat	45549	50999	54871	52797	48257	49594	55359	68083	71888	78397	119163	104723	97161	74383	83450
St. Kitts & Nevis	121069	128829	118153	138686	140145	138557	169820	214632	251523	276714	298968	297757	258189	294481	-
St. Lucia	334162	348947	318737	288408	319997	337486	417944	483673	596820	741737	733045	797410	819165	810305	814521
St. Vincent & the Grenadines	154193	157117	175818	189995	206804	213949	235714	264577	330058	344177	367409	377148	360649	362720	350973

SOURCE: CARICOM Community Secretariat

TABLE 2C
VALUE OF INTRA-REGIONAL TOTAL EXPORTS BY CARICOM COUNTRIES, 1980-1994

CARICOM Countries	1980	1981	1982	1983	1984	1985	1986	1987	1988	1989	1990	1991	1992	1993	1994
CARICOM	1427895	1504453	1479898	1353590	1238551	1251242	840050	868447	1038534	1274984	1374670	1234424	1256168	1423877	1672669
MDCs	1274744	1329124	1270587	1110612	1001620	1016130	616991	665502	776494	1022576	1120862	997546	1018713	1224132	1499077
Barbados	144974	163467	190624	187628	237422	216727	129700	101017	127846	167215	178063	182929	176302	190716	165235
Guyana	144743	161599	116716	86612	68293	50504	33778	27629	28172	36506	36519	-	-	-	-
Jamaica	154227	185505	212215	264493	146124	110414	113120	123154	159719	182256	191735	169444	162054	161595	156743
Trinidad & Tobago	830800	818553	751032	571879	549781	638485	340393	413702	460757	641599	714545	645173	680357	871821	1177099
LDCs	153151	175329	209311	242978	236931	235112	223039	202945	262040	247408	255808	236878	237455	198745	173592
Belize	16285	8331	19454	26050	18804	9180	4227	21665	22380	23391	23111	19396	16423	13100	13508
OECs	13686	166998	189857	216928	218127	225932	218832	181280	239660	224017	232697	217482	221032	186645	160084
Antigua & Barbuda	43088	41399	31002	37996	26639	25321	21237	21735	26735	27078	29993	28723	21115	-	-
Dominica	16171	22196	29851	36377	31881	29385	30537	31716	31670	35715	37551	38096	42762	38588	43334
Grenada	6281	11329	15884	19531	17744	21768	18956	12893	18279	16481	18712	22409	16734	17736	-
Montserrat	1076	2335	1975	2775	2171	762	525	627	335	236	1589	1088	2318	2227	1631
St. Kitts & Nevis	11586	10509	11163	12040	12049	16479	9881	7457	7288	6846	9698	9234	8353	-	-
St. Lucia	40614	49901	48984	45527	35251	27695	37642	45769	59414	6272	58622	50125	42270	56052	39450
St. Vincent & the Grenadines	18050	29329	50998	62682	92392	104522	100054	61083	95939	74689	76532	67807	87480	72042	75669

SOURCE: CARICOM Community Secretariat

TABLE 2D
VALUE OF INTRA-REGIONAL IMPORTS BY CARICOM COUNTRIES, 1980-1994

CARICOM Countries	1980	1981	1982	1983	1984	1985	1986	1987	1988	1989	1990	1991	1992	1993	1994
CARICOM	1411572	1615386	1540642	1371170	1204307	1141577	811142	858276	990044	1255146	1325399	1315381	1379240	1357367	1511307
MDCs	1055589	1277088	1238022	1086942	916303	531353	508608	527604	596816	794307	813195	771682	771190	892315	1029581
Barbados	269282	245803	219531	206332	208914	238752	170049	193415	219773	248700	295551	274730	269338	292364	316888
Guyana	253609	385359	310059	215113	228938	213760	89575	35136	39033	99856	66788	94746	116825	146612	147121
Jamaica	2311253	301559	247288	184605	99374	114703	86430	159204	151003	245143	236842	182460	177933	311617	402627
Trinidad & Tobago	301445	344367	46114	480892	379077	264140	162554	139849	187007	200608	214014	219746	207094	141722	162945
LDCs	355983	338298	302620	284228	288004	310222	302534	330674	393228	460839	512204	543699	608050	465052	481726
Belize	6460	8464	6375	5194	5261	6148	7109	9137	22677	27571	35072	18594	29159	29243	30317
OECs	349523	329834	296245	279034	282743	304074	293425	321537	370351	433268	477132	525105	578891	435809	451409
Antigua & Barbuda	116166	94553	76588	79908	80410	83592	58039	47058	59339	75343	67853	72654	92890		-
Dominica	34501	36056	34912	32862	32732	37023	38546	54245	62528	57134	67749	71006	72319	64825	76304
Grenada	44510	46393	45759	38662	37306	42364	48976	48712	52165	61021	69492	74756	95527	107817	91645
Montserrat	11690	11119	11217	10714	11248	10337	9254	12926	14761	14575	21229	25722	22140	18305	18602
St. Kitts & Nevis	25492	25897	23214	25891	27377	27091	31063	35614	36124	43057	43020	54192	47589		-
St. Lucia	72346	73463	61315	48555	53857	64593	65814	72178	93163	117026	131527	137623	156456	158374	172481
St. Vincent & the Grenadines	44818	42353	43240	42442	39813	39074	43733	50804	52471	65112	76262	89152	91970	86488	92377

SOURCE: CARICOM Community Secreariat

TABLE 3A
INFORMATION RECENT TO CARIBBEAN DEVELOPMENT BANK (US$)

	1991	1992	1993	1994	1995
Approvals			No.		
No. of Capital Projects (New)					
Approved for Loan Financing	18	12	15	8	19
Of which OCR nvolved in	14	11	12	5	15
No. of Additional, Technical Assistance					
and Contingent Loans and Equity	10	9	4	9	4
			$ mn		
Loans Approved for Capital Projects					
(New, Additional and Contingent)	108.9	79.5	91.5	53.4	107.7
Of which OCR accounted for	72.3	52.6	45.8	32.5	83.1
Loans (Net) Approved for Capital					
Projects (New, Additional and Contingent)	101.2	108.7	70.2	42.2	92.4
Amounts Approved for Grants (net)	2.8	19.8	1.1	3.1	1.5
Disbursements[1]			$ mn		
Amount Disbursed in OCR &					
Venezuelan Trust Fund (VTF)	20.7	27.9	22.5	26.5	30.9
Amount Disbursed in SFR	33.1	33	25.8	24.5	20.4
Total Disbursed	53.8	60.9	48.3	51.0	51.3
Net Transfers	(2.1)	1.3	-11.1	-14.3	-15.6
Portfolio			$ mn		
OCR Loans Outstanding	165.5	177.4	188	204.9	219.2
VTF Loans Outstanding	4.8	4.1	3.4	2.2	1.5
SFR Loans Outstanding	349.5	348.3	346.4	344.0	342.3
Total Loans Outstanding	519.8	529.8	537.8	551.1	563
Financial Performance			$ mn		
Net Income on OCR[2]	12.4	13.6	12.8	11.8	15.5
Net Income on SFR[2]	7.6	6.6	4.1	6.4	11.9
Total Net Income	20.0	20.2	16.9	18.2	27.4
Supervision			No.		
Projects under Supervision	273	299	302	282	
Projects under Implementation[3]	95	118	105	105	
Projects Operational[4]	178	181	197	177	
Financial Intermediaries	27	19	20	20	
Administration					
Total Staff in place at Dec. 31 (No.)	186	189	187	184	
Total Administrative Expenses ($mn)	8.5	9	9.6	10.2	10.6
Administrative Expenses to Total Average					
Loans Outstanding (%)	1.7	1.7	1.8	1.9	1.9

1 Translated at rates effective at December 31 of each year
2 Shown at hiostorical exchange rates and before appropriations
3 Includes lines of credit not fully disbursed.
4 Excludes lines of credit.

SOURCES: Caribbean Development Bank

Appendix B / 129

TABLE 3B
SELECTED ECONOMIC INDICATORS ON CDBs BORROWING MEMBER COUNTRIES

Country	SDF 1/ Classification	Area (km2)	Mid-year Population 1994 ('000)	Annual Rate of Population Increases 1991-94 %	Annual Change in Consumer Prices 1994 %	GDP at Current Market Prices 1993 ($mn)	GDP at Current Market Prices 1994 ($mn)	GDP Per Capita at Current Prices 1994 ($)	Real Rate of Growth in GDP 1994 ($)
MDCs (Total / Average)		245896	5057.5	0.9	-	14185.3	14609.5	2889	-
Bahamas	I	13942	270	1.4	1.3	3191.2	3252.9	12048	0.6
Barbados	I	432	264.3	0.3	0.6	1650.6	1738.6	6578	4
Guyana	IV	214970	797.1	1.2	16.1	466.5	540.2	704	8
Jamaica	III	11424	2498.8	1	35.1	4207.5	4241.4	1697	0.8
Trinidad & Tobago	I	5128	1257.3	0.4	8.8	4669.5	4836.4	3847	4
LDCs (Total / Average)		26792	819	1.5		3674.5	3870.2	4725	
Belize	III	22960	209	2.5	2.3	524.6	552.3	2642	2.5
OECs (Total / Average)		2910	537.2	0.7		1911.4	2014.6	3750	
Antigua and Barbuda	II	440	64.2	1.2	3.5	456.9	494.5	7702	5.3
Dominica	III	750	73.5	1	2	201.6	207.7	2825	1.8
Grenada	III	345	97	0.5	2.6	257.4	272.6	2810	2
Montserrat	III	102	10.4	1.1	2.8	58.5	60.8	5846	0.8
St. Kitts & Nevis	III	269	42	0.1	3.5	197.6	209.3	4982	3
St. Lucia	III	616	142.7	1.6	2.2	497.2	513.1	3596	2.2
St. Vincent and the Grenadines	III	388	107.4	0.3	0.7	242.2	256.7	2390	2
Other LDCs (Total/Average)		922	72.8	3.9		1238.5	1303.3	17896	
Anguilla	II	91	9.9	4.2	4	55.4	61.1	6153	7
British Virgin Islands	II	150	17	0.7	4.2	242	277.3	16312	3.5
Cayman Islands	I	264	31.3	4.3	3.1	852.9	871.2	27835	5.3
Turks and Caicos Islands	III	417	14.6	6.3		88.2	93.7	6418	1.4
All Countries (Total/Average)		272688	5876.6	1.0	-	17859.8	18479.6	3145	-

SOURCE: Caribbean Development Bank

TABLE 3C
SELECTED ECONOMIC INDICATORS ON CDBs BORROWING MEMBER COUNTRIES

Country	SDF 1/ Classification	Rate of Growth in GDP 1991-1993 (%)	Value Added in Agriculture as % GDP 1992-1994	Value Added in Mining as % GDP 1992-1994	Value Added in Manufacturing as % GDP 1992-1994	Value Added in Construction as % GDP 1992-1994	Gross Domestic Savings as % GDP 1992-1994	Gross Domestic Investment as % GDP 1992-1994	Central Government Recurrent Revenue as % GDP 1994	Central Government Recurrent Expenditure as % GDP 1994
MDCs (Total /Average)									26.2	24.8
Bahamas	I	-	-	-	-	-	-	-	19.7	17.4
Barbados	I	2.4	6.4	1.7	8.7	5.2	17.3	12.2	29.3	27.3
Guyana	IV	8.0	49.2	21.2	4.6	4.0	37.6	50.3	36.0	36.4
Jamaica	III	1.4	7.3	8.0	19.8	13.1	25.5	31.8	28.7	27.6
Trinidad & Tobago	I	1.7	2.4	23.7	9.1	7.6	22.6	12.8	26.2	25.3
LDCs (Total /Average)									24.2	22.4
Belize	III	7.3	25.0	0.8	19.3	10.4	20.6	29.1	23.9	24.4
OECs (Total/Average)									25.8	23.9
Antigua and Barbuda	II	2.4	11.1	0.8	7.1	10.0	14.6	23.7	21.4	22.9
Dominica	III	2.3	4.2	1.7	2.6	10.3	20.9	21.8	27.8	28.1
Grenada	III	1.1	21.7	0.8	8.4	8.1	1.7	16.0	23.0	22.0
Montserrat	III	2.1	11.8	0.5	8.1	8.7	15.3	30.5	25.7	24.9
St. Kitts & Nevis	III	3.8	5.4	1.2	2.7	10.4	5.9	37.5	25.4	24.8
St. Lucia	III	4.6	7.3	0.4	12.4	12.9	27.2	38.8	25.3	19.3
St. Vincent &the Grenadines	III	3.9	12.0	0.6	7.5	9.0	10.2	15.9	26.7	23.0
			17.7	0.3	9.8	11.5	13.0	26.8		
Other LDCs (Total/Average)									23.8	21.0
Anguilla	II	7.4	4.7	-	-	17.9	9.4	35.3	24.0	23.7
British Virgin Islands	II	3.1	3.8	0.9	0.8	8.5	12.0	54.4	30.2	24.5
Cayman Islands	I	4.9	-	0.2	3.9	-	-	-	20.7	18.5
Turks and Caicos Islands	III	5.2	4.6	1.4	0.4	8.6	24.4	40.0	33.9	32.4
All Countries (Total/Average)		-	-	-	-	-	-	-	25.8	24.3

SOURCE: Caribbean Development Bank

Appendix B / 131

TABLE 3D: SELECTED ECONOMIC INDICATORS ON CDBs BORROWING MEMBER COUNTRIES

Country	Central Government Recurrent Account Surplus as % GDP 1994	Export of Goods & Services 1994 ($mn)	Import of Goods & Services 1994 ($mn)	Tourist Expenditure 1994 ($mn)	Balance of Payments Current Account 1994 ($mn)	Change in Net Foreign Assets 2/ December 1994 ($mn)	Disbursed & Outstanding External Public Debt Dec. 1994 ($mn)	Scheduled Debt Service Payments on External Public Debt Dec. 1994 ($mn)	Ratio of Debt Service Payments to Exports of Goods and Services 1994 ($mn)
MDCs (Total /Average)									
Bahamas	1.4	7767.7	—	2976.4	255.5	389.9	8560.8	1412.5	18.2
Barbados	2.4	1789.2	1974.6	1332.6	32.4	(18.3)	410.5	93.7	5.2
Guyana	2.0	1003.4	866.6	597.6	123.7	31.2	442.0	105.3	10.5
Jamaica	(0.4)	526.4	—	47.0	(100.8)	(21.7)	2004.0	99.2	18.8
Trinidad & Tobago	1.1	2453.8	2791.9	919.0	116.6	0.0	3651.8	536.1	21.8
	0.9	1994.9	—	80.2	83.6	398.7	2052.5	578.2	29.0
LDCs (Total /Average)	1.8	—	—	1552.2	—	—	951.3	76.6	—
Belize	(0.5)	292.9	346.2	75.0	(24.6)	(7.3)	180.4	24.0	8.2
OECs (Total/Average)	1.9	1244.9	1578.4	853.2	(178.2)	(5.7)	663.7	40.3	3.2
Antigua & Barbuda	(1.5)	440.8	463.9	394.0	(18.0)	7.5	240.2	6.0	1.4
Dominica	(0.3)	95.6	145.7	30.6	(38.8)	(4.7)	102.3	7.4	7.7
Grenada	1.0	127.7	180.4	59.3	(32.9)	15.4	79.3	5.3	4.2
Montserrat	0.8	30.1	48.8	18.5	(12.3)	5.2	10.3	0.5	1.8
St. Kitts & Nevis	0.6	120.2	159.7	76.2	(27.2)	(10.6)	45.3	4.9	4.1
St. Lucia & the Grenadines	6.1	336.9	407.9	224.1	12.2	(16.0)	105.2	10.3	3.1
St. Vincent	3.7	93.7	172.0	50.5	(61.3)	(2.4)	81.1	5.9	6.3
Other LDCs (Total/Average)	2.8	—	—	624.0	—	—	107.2	12.3	—
Anguilla	0.2	—	—	51.0	(10.3)	11.4	14.0	0.6	0.9
British Virgin Islands	5.8	63.2	73.5	188.2	—	—	34.5	2.5	1.6
Cayman Islands	2.1	159.3	272.5	328.3	—	—	54.6	8.6	—
Turks and Caicos Islands	1.5	63.0	63.5	56.5	—	—	4.1	0.6	1.0
All Countries (Total/Average)	1.5	—	—	4528.6	—	—	9512.1	1489.1	—

Notes: — = not available (cannot be derived)
1/ SDF Classification is based on eligibility of resources under SDF 3 and creditworthiness; 2/ ( ) denotes decline

SOURCE: Caribbean Development Bank

TABLE 3E
SELECTED ECONOMIC INDICATORS ON CDBs BORROWING MEMBER COUNTRIES

Selected Labour Force Indicators* 1994

	Participation Rates (%)			Labour Force Unemployment Rates (%)			Employment by Sector (%)			
	Male	Female	Both Sexes	Male	Female	Both Sexes	Agriculture	Mining/ Quarrying	Manufacturing	Construction
Barbados	74.5	61.1	67.2	17.3	26.4	21.8	5.7	-ᵃ	10.9	8.3
Jamaica	74.6	62.4	68.5	9.6	21.8	15.4	23.6	0.7	10.3	7.2
Montserrat	-	-	-	-	-	8.3	7.4	0.3	3.9	29.0
St Luciaᵇ	-	-	66.7	14.6	24.7	19.2	25.7	-	12.1	8.6
Trinidad & Tobago	-	-	59.1	16.3	22.4	18.6	12.9	3.7	10.0	12.0

a - included in construction
b - January to June only
* - For those countries having relevant data

SOURCE: Caribbean Development Bank

APPENDIX C

Some Formal Statements on CARICOM by Heads of Government and State

Adams, J.M.G,. Address at Symposium on Ten Years of CARICOM, 1983

Arthur, Owen, CARICOM Chairman's Statement at Miami Summit, 1994

Barrow, Errol, Address at Opening of CARICOM Summit in Guyana (CARICOM Secretariat), 1986

———— Chairman's Statement to Meeting of CDB Board of Governors, 1975

Bird, Vere, Chairman's Opening Statement at CARICOM Heads of Government Conference (CARICOM Secretariat), 1988

Blaize, Herbert, Chairman's Opening Statement at CARICOM Heads of Government Conference (CARICOM Secretariat), 1989

Chambers, George, Opening Statement at CARICOM Heads of Government Conference (CARICOM Secretariat), 1983

Compton John, Statement at CDB Annual Meeting of Board of Governors (Belize), 1994

———— Chairman's Opening Statement at CARICOM Heads of Government Conference (CARICOM Secretariat), 1987

———— Statement at Formal Launching of the West Indian Commission (Port-of-Spain), 1990

Esquivel, Manuel, Opening Address at CDB Board of Governors Meeting (Belize), 1994

Hoyte, Desmond, Opening Address at CARICOM Heads of Government Conference (CARICOM Secretariat), 1986

Ingraham, Hubert, Chairman's Opening Address at CARICOM Heads of Government Conference (CARICOM Secretariat), 1993

Jagan, Cheddi, Opening Statement at CARICOM Heads of Government Conference (CARICOM Secretariat), 1992

_____Statement to Miami Summit, 1994

Manley, Michael, Opening Address at CARICOM Heads of Government Conference (Grand Anse, Grenada) (CARICOM Secretariat), 1989

_____Chairman's Opening Remarks at CARICOM Heads of Government Conference (CARICOM Secretariat), 1990

Manning, Patrick, Chairman's Opening Statement at CARICOM Heads of Government Conference (CARICOM Secretariat), 1992

Meade, Reuben, Meeting of CDB Board of Governors, 1994

Patterson, Percival, Chairman's Opening Statement at CARICOM Heads of Government Conference (CARICOM Secretariat), 1994

Pindling, Lynden, Chairman's Opening Statement at CARICOM Heads of Government Conference (CARICOM Secretariat), 1984

Price, George, Opening Statement at CARICOM Heads of Government Conference (Jamaica), 1990

Robinson, A.N.R., Statement at CARICOM Heads of Government Conference, 1987

_____Chairman's Address at Formal Launching of West Indian Commission, 1990

Sandiford, Erskine, Opening Address at CARICOM Heads of Government Conference (CARICOM Secretariat) (Kingston), 1991

Seaga, Edward, Chairman's Opening Statement at CARICOM Heads of Government Conference (CARICOM Secretariat), 1982

Simmonds, Kennedy, Opening Statement at CARICOM Heads of Government Conference (CARICOM Secretariat), 1991

St John, Bernard, Opening Address at CARICOM Heads of Government Conference (CARICOM Secretariat), 1985

APPENDIX D

References and Additional Material

Abrams, Elliot, *The Shiprider Solution: Policing the Caribbean*, Hudson Institute, Spring 1996

Alleyne, George, *Health and Development: Caribbean Perspective* (Eric Williams Memorial Lecture)

Barsotti, Frank, 'Entering the 21st Century', *Caribbean Quarterly*, 1st Quarter 1990

Beckford, George, *Development in Suspense. Selected Papers and Proceedings of the 1st Conference of the Association of Caribbean Economists*, FES Kingston

_____Plantations and Poverty, OUP, 1977

Benn, Dennis, *The State and The Private Sector in Caribbean Development*, UNDP, 1993

Bennett, Karl, *Monetary Arrangements in CARICOM*. (Adlith Brown Memorial Lecture) 1991.

Best, Lloyd, Girvan, Norman, Thomas, Clive and Ramsaran, Ramesh, *Economic Liberalization and Caribbean Development*, ISER, St Augustine, 1994

_____ *International Co-operation in the Industrialization Process: The Case of Trinidad and Tobago*, UNIDO, Industry 2000, 198

_____ Lloyd, *Introduction to Caribbean Monetary Integration* CIS, Port-of-Spain, 1994

_____ *Trade and Macro-economic Policies and Structural Adjustment in relation to Regional Economic Integration*, CARICOM Secretariat, 1994

_____ Lloyd, *Independent Thought and Caribbean Freedom: Revisited after Thirty Years* (Cultural Conference in Honour of Rex Nettleford), UWI, 1996.

Birdsall, Nancy, Economic Development Is Social Development, 1992

Bisnauth, Dale, *Cultural Dimensions of West Indian Structural Process in Small Open Economies*, CARICOM Secretariat, 1992

Blackman, Courtney, 'Toward a Monetary Union', *Caribbean Affairs*, 2nd Quarter, 1986

Blake, Byron, *The International Monetary Fund and the Structural Adjustment Process in Small Open Economies*

_____ *The Role of Small Businesses in the Caribbean Economy*, CARICOM Secretariat, 1984

_____ *Production, Integration: Scope, Limitations and Prospects in CARICOM in Ten Years of CARICOM*, 1983

Boxill, Ian, *An Ideology of Caribbean Integration*, UWI, 1993

Brewster, Havelock, and Thomas, Clive, *The Dynamics of West Indian Integration*, ISER, UWI

_____ Havelock, *The Caribbean Community in a Changing International Environment: Toward the Next Century* (Adlith Brown Memorial Lecture), UWI, 1992

_____ *The Report of the West Indian Commission: Time for Action. Critique and Agenda for Further Work* (Mimeo), 1993

_____ *Social Capital and Development: Reflections on Barbados and Jamaica*, 1996

Caribbean Community Secretariat, *The Treaty of Chaguaramas. Establishing the Caribbean Community*, CARICOM Secretariat, 1973

_____ (ed.) *Ten Years of CARICOM*, CARICOM Secretariat, 1983

Carlsson, Ingvar and Ramphal, Shridath (co-chairmen), *Report of the Commission on Global Governance*, Geneva, 1995

Carrington, Edwin, *Practical Agenda for Re-vitalising the Caribbean Community*

_____ CARICOM and the Association of Caribbean States, *Politica Internacional*, Caracas, April-June 1994

_____ *The Caribbean: Facing up to the twenty-first century*, Institute of International Relations, UWI, 1996

Chernick, Sidney, *The Commonwealth Caribbean: The Integration Experience*, World Bank, 1978

Chevannes, Barrington, *Rastafari: Roots and Ideology*, Syracuse UWI Press, 1994

Commonwealth Secretariat, *Vulnerability: Small States in the Global Society*, 1985

Cummings, Christine, *Beyond the Boundaries: Reviewing the Administration of West Indies Cricket* (UWI/Conference in honour of Rex Nettleford), 1996

Davies, Omar, 'The Jamaican Economy Since Independence: Agenda for the Future' in *Jamaica: Preparing for the twenty-first Century*,' PIOJ, 1994

Demas, William, *Towards West Indian Survival*, WIC, 1990

_____ *Essays on Caribbean Integration and Development*, Mona, UWI, 1976

_____ *Consolidating Our Independence. The Major Challenge Facing the West Indies*, IIP, St Augustine, 1986

Downes, Andrew, 'Structural Adjustment and the Private Sector' *Caribbean Affairs*, 3rd Quarter, 1992

Downes, Andrew (with T. Barker and J. Sackey), *Perspectives on Economic Development: Essays on W. Arthur Lewis*, University Press of America, 1980

_____ *Twenty-five years of West Indies Cricket: From Sobers to Lara*, UWI, 1996

Dumas, Reginal, 'Ten Issues for the Summit', *Caribbean Affairs*, July-August 1994

_____ In the Service of the Public Press) 1995

Emmanuel, Patrick, *Approaches to Caribbean Political Integration*, UWI, Cave Hill, 1987.

_____*Community within a Community: the OECS Countries*

Emtage, Steve, *Savings and Investment in Barbados*, Regional Programme of Monetary Studies, 1987

Farrell, Trevor, *Size and Development* (Grenada Conference on Small States), 1991

_____ *The Concept of Small States. Current Problems and Future Prospects (with Special Reference to the Caribbean)*

_____ *Conference on Small States* sponsored by ECCB, March 1991

Farrell, Terrence and Worrell, Delisle (ed.) *Caribbean Monetary Integration*, CIS, Port-of-Spain, 1994

Figueroa, Mark, 'The Plantation School and Lewis: Contradictions, Continuities and Continued Caribbean Relevance'. Paper Presented to Symposium on The Plantation Economy Model 25 Years Later, Department of Economics, UWI St Augustine, April 7-8, 1994.

_____ Does the Market Undermine its Social Resource Base? UWI, March 1996

Francis, A.A., Taxation on Bauxite/Alumina in Jamaica

Francis, Fitz, *Some Fundamental Issues Associated with Implementation of Fiscal Policy in CARICOM Member States*, OECS, 1985

Ghany, Hamid, 'The Myth of the Westminster Model', *Caribbean Affairs*, July-August 1994

Gill, Henry, *CARICOM and the wider Caribbean and Latin America*, WIC, 1992

_____ 'An Examination of the ACS Convention' (unpublished), 1994

Girvan, Norman, 'A Strategic Approach to Technology', in Jamaica, Ian Randle Publishers, Jamaica, 1994

_____ 'Eight Lessons of Liberalisation in Jamaica', in Jamaica, Ian Randle Publishers, Jamaica, 1994

_____ Boxill, Ian, Whitehead, Judy, Samuel, Wendell, *The Integration of Production in CARICOM*, Consortium Graduate School, Mona, UWI, (Mimeo), 1994

_____ *Planning for the 21st Century: A 2020 View*, PIOJ, 1995

Girvan, Norman, Beckford, George *Development in Suspense. Selected Papers and Proceedings of the 1st Conference of the Caribbean Economists*, FES,

_____ *A Strategic Approach to Technology. Jamaica Preparing for the Twenty-first Century*, PIOJ, 1994

_____ Jefferson, Owen (ed.) *Readings in Caribbean Political Economy*, ISER, Mona, 1971

Gonzales, Anthony, *CARICOM and Venezuela: Trade and Investment*, Andrew Mellon Foundation, 1994

_____ *Caribbean/EEC Cooperation: Towards a post-Lomé Strategy*, North-South Centre, 1993

Government of Barbados, *Protocol for the Implementation of a Prices and Income Policy, 1995-1997*, Bridgetown, 1995

Government of Jamaica, *White Paper on National Industrial Policy*, Kingston, March 1996

_____ Proposal on

Grimshaw, Anna, *C.L.R. James Readings*, OUP, 1993

Group of Caribbean Experts, *The Caribbean Community in the 1980s*, CARICOM Secretariat, 1983

Hall, Stuart, *Cultural Identity in the Diaspora*, (Address at Cultural Conference in Honour of Rex Nettleford), UWI, 1996

Harewood, Ainsworth, 'Caribbean Monetary Integration', *Caribbean Affairs*, July/August 1994

Harris, Donald, 'The Jamaican Economy in the 21st century: Challenges to Development and Requirements of a response', in Jamaica, Ian Randle Publishers, Jamaica, 1994

Hartwich, Dieter, *Europe as a Source of Investment for the Caribbean. Meeting on Financing the New Caribbean*, UWI, 1994

_____ "Cooperation in Human Resource Development in the Commonwealth 'Caribbean'", *Bulletin of Eastern Caribbean Affairs*, Bridgetown, 1990

Holder, Jean, *Changing role of National Tourism Organisation*, Caribbean Tourism Organisation, 1992

Iglesias, Enrique, *Remarks at the Miami Hemispheric Summit by the President of the IDB*, 1994

Jagan, Cheddi, *The Caribbean Community: Crossroads to the Future*, UWI, St Augustine, 1994

James, C.L.R., *Beyond a Boundary*, Macmillan, New York, 1963

Jefferson, Owen, Liberalisation of the Foreign Exchange System in Jamaica (Adlith Brown Memorial Lecture)

Jones, Edwin, *Development Administration: Some Jamaican Adaptations*, Kingston, CARICOM Publishers, 1992

Jones, Hendrickson, *Public Finance and Monetary Policy in Small, Open Economies*, ISER, UWI, 1985

Knight, Franklin, *The Caribbean: The Genesis of a Fragmented Nationalism*, OUP, 2nd Edn, 1991

_____ 'New Caribbean and the United States' *Annals of the American Academy of Political and Social Sciences*, 1994

Lamming, George, *Opening Address at UWI Cultural Conference*, 1996

_____ *Coming, Coming Home: Conversation II*, St Martin, 1995

Lalor, Dennis, *UWI Graduation Address at Mona Campus*, October 1993

Le Franc, Elsie, (ed.), *Consequences of Structural Adjustment: A Review of The Jamaican Experience*, University of the West Indies Press, 1994

Lestrade, Swinburne, *CARICOM's Less Developed Countries: A Review of the Progress of LDC. within the CARICOM*, Cave Hill, UWI, 1981

Levitt, Kari, *Debt, Adjustment and Development*, (Eric Williams Memorial Lecture), Central Bank of Trinidad and Tobago, 1990

_____ *The Origins and Consequences of the Debt Crisis with Special Emphasis on the External Sector from 1983 to 1988*, Conference of Caribbean Economists, Bridgetown, 1989

_____ *From Decolonisation to Neo-Liberalism* (Beckford Memorial Lecture), 1996

_____ Kari, with Best, Lloyd 'A model of Plantation Economy', George Beckford (ed.), *Caribbean Economy*

Lewis, J. O'Neil, 'Some thoughts on Caribbean Integration Past and Present' *Caribbean Affairs*, 1985

Lewis, Arthur, 'The Agony of the Eight', *Barbados Advocate*, 1965

_____ *Theory of Economic Growth*, Allen and Unwin, 1955

_____ *President's Statement to the 1972 Meeting of the Board of Governors of the Caribbean Development Bank*

_____ ,with Wording, Hugh, *et al.*, 'Towards an Eastern Caribbean Federation' *BIM Magazine*, Bridgetown,

_____ *Development Planning*, Allen and Unwin, 1966

Lewis, Vaughan, *Size, Self Determination and International Relations. The Caribbean*, Mona, UWI, Mona, ISER, 1988

_____ The Commonwealth Caribbean and Self-Determination

_____ *Compulsions of Integration*, West Indian Commission Occasional Papers, 1992

_____, with McIntyre, Alister and Emmanuel, Patrick, *The Politics of Independence in the Windward and Leeward Islands*, 1983

Maingot, Anthony, *The United States and the Caribbean*, Macmillan Caribbean, 1994

McBain, Helen, 'The South at the End of the Twentieth Century', *Structural Change in the Caribbean Compared: Graduation or Marginalisation in World Economy*, Swatuck, Larry and Shaw, Timothy M. eds., Macmillan, 1994

McDonald, Ian, 'To be a West Indian: A Personal View of the Integration Movement' Georgetown 1990, presented at UWI St Augustine, March 29, 1990

McIntyre, Alister, *Trade Policy For the West Indies*, New World, 1974

_____ *The University Revisited* (Eric Williams Memorial Lecture, Central Bank of Trinidad and Tobago), 1989

_____ 'The Importance of Negotiation Preparedness: Reflections on the Caribbean Experience', *Dialogue*, ISER, Vol. 1 No.1, July-August 1976

_____ *Human Resource Development: Its Reference to Jamaica and the Caribbean*, Kingston 1990

_____ *The Future of CARICOM in the Global Economy. Jamaica Preparing for the twenty-first century.*

_____ Lewis, Vaughan and Emmanuel, Patrick, *The Political Economy. Integration in the Leeward and Windward Islands*, 1983

McIntyre, Arnold, *Investment, Trade and Development Issues in The Caribbean*, WIC,

Manley, Michael, 'The Integration Movement', *Caribbean Quarterly*, 1st Quarter, 1988

_____ *History of West Indies Cricket*, André Deutsh, London

_____ *Up the Down Escalator*, Howard University Press

Miller, Errol, *Education and Society in the Commonwealth Caribbean*, ISER, UWI, Mona, 1991

Mills, Don and Lewis, Vaughan, 'Caribbean-Latin American Relations' (Unpublished)

Mills, Gladstone, Burton, C, Lewis, J. O'Neil, Sorhaindo, C., *Report on a Comprehensive review of Programmes, Institutions and Organisations of CARICOM*, CARICOM Secretariat,

Mitchell, James, *Two Decades of Caribbean Unity*, Kingstown, St Vincent, 1987

_____ *Caribbean Crusade*, Kingstown, St Vincent, 1991

Mohammed, Kamaluddin, *Caribbean Integration*, Port-of-Spain, 1969

Mullings, Rupert, *A Practical Monetary System for CARICOM countries*, CDB, 1979

_____ *The Caribbean Development Bank and the Adjustment Process*, London, 1982.

Naipaul, Vidia, *The Mimic Men*, André Deutsch, London, 1967

_____ *The Middle Passage*, André Deutsch, London, 1962

Nettleford, Rex, *Caribbean Identity in the World of Ideas*, Commonwealth Secretariat, London, 1986

_____ Closing Address at UWI Cultural Conference, UWI, 1996

_____ *Memories of Emancipation; Lessons and The Legacies*, UWI, 1994

_____ *Inward Grasp, Outward Reach*, UWI, 1995

Nicholls, Neville, *Co-operation in the Wider Caribbean* (CDB President's Statement at the Board of Governors Meeting), 1991

_____ *Commonwealth Caribbean at Another Crossroad* (CDB Board of Governors' Meeting), 1991

_____ Sustaining Development in the Commonwealth Caribbean (President's Statement at Annual Meeting of CDB Board of Governors Meeting) 1993

Panday, Basdeo, Opening Address (Conference on Europe and the Caribbean Council), Port-of-Spain, 1995

Pantin, Dennis, *Foreign Debt* (CSA Conference), 1989

Panton, David, 'The Case for a Caribbean Court of Appeal', *The Gleaner*, October 26, 1990

Patterson, P.J., Opening lecture of Carl Stone Series, UWI, Mona, 1994

_____ Intervention Issues Affecting Caribbean Development (Meeting on Financing the New Caribbean), UWI, 1994

Payne, Anthony and Sutton, Paul, *Caribbean International Relations Beyond 1992: Europe and North America*, WIC, 1992

Persaud, Bishnodat, *Sustainable Development in the Caribbean*, UWI, 1994

_____ *Investment and Trade. Enhancing the Development Effort.* (Round Table Oxford Conference) September 28-29, 1993.

Planning Institute of Jamaica (ed.) *Jamaica preparing for the 21st Century*, Ian Randle Publishers, Jamaica, 1994

Poon, Auliana, *Tourism: An Axial Product* WIC, 1992

Ragnauth, Bishnu, with Foreword by Norman Girvan, *Tribute to a Scholar: Appreciating CLR James*, Consortium Graduate School, Mona, 1990

Rainford, Roderick, *Regional Economic Planning and Development for the Caribbean: The Management Imperative*, St Augustine, UWI, 1987

_____ *Towards An Integrated Single Market in the Caribbean Community*, CARICOM Secretariat, 1992

_____ Banking in an Environment of Liberalised Capital Flows, ECCB, 1995

Ramchand, Kenneth, *Acts of Possession: The New World of the West Indian Writers* (Eric Williams Memorial Lecture), Central Bank of Trinidad and Tobago, 1991

Rampersad, Frank, *Implications of the Uruguay Round for the CARICOM Countries*, Ian Randle Publishers, Kingston, 1996

_____ What Next for Caribbean Integration? A Statement at the Symposium on Caribbean-United States Relations, Institute of International Relations, UWI, May 21, 1992

_____ with Gill, H., Hosten-Graig, H., and Gonzales, A. *Implications of NAFTA for the CARICOM region and a proposed response*, CARICOM, 1994

Ramphal, Shridath, *To Care for CARICOM*, CARICOM Secretariat, 1975

_____ *Options For the Caribbean. The Lure of Realpolitik*, Institute of IR, UWI, St Augustine, 1987

_____ Global Governance and New Dimensions of Human Security (Sir John Crawford Management Lecture), Washington, DC, 1995

_____ 'The University in the 1990s: Finding Ways to Reduce the Knowledge Gap', *Caribbean Affairs*, 1st Quarter 1992

_____ and Carlsson (co-Chairmen), *Report of the Commission on Global Governance*, Geneva, 1995

Ramsaran, Ramesh, *Commonwealth Caribbean in the World Economy*, Warwick University Caribbean Institute

_____ (ed.) *Economic Liberalisation and Caribbean Development*. Articles Lloyd Best, Norman Girvan and Clive Thomas, ISER, St Augustine, 1994.

_____ *Some Issues and Problems with the Development of the Financial Structure in post-Independence Trinidad and Tobago* (Conference on Financing Development in the Caribbean Regional Programme of Monetary Studies, Barbados), 1989

_____ *Epilogue: Facts and Fallacy in Economic Liberalization*

Reid, George, *Evolving Structure of the CARICOM Trade Regime*, 1985

_____ *Jamaica and the World Bank in the Mid-eighties*, Bridgetown, 1995

Robinson, A.N.R., Future of the Caribbean (Royal Institute of International Affairs), London, October 1988

_____ *The Future of Caribbean Economies. Integration in a Hemispheric Context.* (Mimeo.) 194, Warwick University, Caribbean Studies, Macmillan, 1989

Robinson, John M., *The Future of Caribbean Economic Integration in the Hemispheric Context*, (IDB-sponsored Conference on WIC Report), 1992

Robotham, Donald, *Reflections on a Caribbean Work Ethic. (Restructuring our Economic Alternatives in the Caribbean*, Memphis, 1992

Rohler, Gordon, Presentation (UWI Conference on Caribbean Calling), Mona, 1990

Ryan, Selwyn, 'The Caribbean State in the 21st Century', *Caribbean Affairs*, November, 1990

Samuel, Wendell, with Girvan, Norman, Boxill, Ian, Whitehead, Judy, *The Integration of Production in the Caribbean*, OECS, ECCB

_____ Trade Unions under the Lomé Convention: The Promise and the Disappointment (Symposium on Foreign Trade and Finance in Barbados and the OECS), Cave Hill, Barbados, December 1989

Serwar, Lloyd, *Joint Conduct of External Political Relations and its Effects on the Integration Process In the Ten Years of CARICOM*, 1984

_____ with Gonzales, A., (Structures of Unity For the Caribbean Community) WIC, 1991

Sherlock, Philip, *Role of Education and Modernisation of the Caribbean People*, Contemporary Caribbean Issues, University of Puerto Rico, 1979

Shirley, Gordon, *Technology, Productivity and Global Competitiveness*, Kingston, 1991

Singh, Rickey, 'Positive Vibes as Curtain Falls on CARICOM Summit', *Sunday Sun*, Bridgetown, July 10, 1994

St Rose, Marius, *Likely Global Trends: Possible Implications and Suggested Strategies For The Caribbean*, CDB, 1992

_____ *OECS Prospects, Response and Special Needs*, CDB, 1994

Streeten, Paul, 'The Minimalist State', World Development, 1992

_____ 'The Special Problems of Small Countries' *World Development*, Vol. 21 #2, 1993

Thomas, Clive, 'Lessons From Experience' Structural Adjustment and Poverty in Guyana', SES, Vol. 42 #41, 1993

_____ and Nettleford, Rex, *The University of the West Indies: A Caribbean Response to the Challenge of Change*, London, Macmillan, 1990

_____ *Reflections of Changing Perspective of the West Indian Past* (Eric Williams Memorial Lecture), Central Bank, Port-of-Spain, 1986

_____ *Sugar: Threat or Challenge?*, IDRC, 1985

_____ *Financing Development. The Mobilisation of Savings in Commonwealth Caribbean*, Regional Programme of Monetary Studies, UWI, 1989

_____ 'Adjustment, Stabilisation and Exchange Rates', in *Jamaica*, Ian Randle Publishers, Jamaica, 1994

_____ with Brewster, Havelock, *Dynamics of West Indian Integration*, ISER, 1967

_____ 'Social Capital' *Development*, UWI, Mona, 1996

_____ *The Crisis in Development Theory* (Beckford Lecture), UWI, 1996

Thompson, Patterson, *Strategy of Economic Development and its Integration Process*, CAIC, Barbados, 1990

Treaty establishing the Organization of Eastern Caribbean States (OECS Secretariat), 1983

United Nations ECLAC (CDCC) *Factors Affecting the Participation of the Caribbean Countries in the Free Trade Area of the Americas*, November, 1995

United Nations ECLAC (Head office), *Towards Open Regionalism*, CEPAL Review, 1993

UWI, Report of the Chancellor's *Commission on the Governance of UWI A New Structure – The Regional University in the 1990s and Beyond*, July 1994

UWI, *Summary Report on Financing the New Caribbean*, UWI, 1994

Venner, Dwight, *The State In the Caribbean: With Special Reference to the mini-economy*, Department of Economics, UWI, 1986

Walcott, Derek, *The Antilles: Fragments of Epic Memory* (Nobel Prize Lecture), 1993

Wedderburn, Judith, *Integration and Participatory Development: Selected papers and proceedings of the 2nd Conference of Caribbean Economists*, Kingston, FES, 1994

Weintraub, Sidney, *The Summit and Beyond: Trade Options for the Hemisphere*, Washington, DC, 1994

Whitehead, Judy, et al., *The Integration of Production in CARICOM*, 1994

Williams, Eric, 'The Caribbean Economic Community', *The Nation*, September - November 1965, Port-of-Spain

_____ *From Columbus to Castro*, André Deutsch, London, 1969

_____ *Capitalism and Slavery*, Chapel Hill, 1944

Witter, Michael, *Devaluation and Balance of Payments: The Case of Jamaica*, UWI, Mona,

_____ (ed.) *Caribbean Development and Caribbean People: The Present As History*, Ian Randle Publishers, Jamaica, 1996

Wooding, Hugh, Lewis, Arthur, *et al.*, 'Towards an Eastern Caribbean Federation', *BIM Magazine*, Bridgetown, 1972

Worrell, Delisle, *Economic Integration Between Unequal Partners – North America and the Caribbean*, Central Bank of Barbados, 1994

―――― with Farrell, Terrence, *Caribbean Monetary Integration*, CIS, Port-of-Spain, 1994

―――― *CARICOM Responses to NAFTA*, CARICOM Secretariat, 1994

WORLD BANK, *Caribbean Countries: Policies for Private-Sector Development*, 1994

―――― *Economic Policies for Transition in the OECS*, 1994

―――― *The East Asian Miracle*, World Bank, 1993